Living in Difficult Relationships

Peter M. Kalellis

Paulist Press
New York / Mahwah, NJ

Cover image courtesy of llaszlo/Shutterstock.com
Cover design by Sharyn Banks
Book design by Lynn Else

Library of Congress Cataloging-in-Publication Data

Kalellis, Peter M.
    Living in difficult relationships / Peter M. Kalellis.
        p. cm.
    Includes bibliographical references (p.   ).
    ISBN 978-0-8091-4764-9 (alk. paper) — ISBN 978-1-61643-139-6 1. Interpersonal relations—Religious aspects—Christianity. 2. Marriage—Religious aspects—Christianity. I. Title.
    BV4597.52.K355 2012
    248.8'44—dc23

                                                                2011049350

Published by Paulist Press
997 Macarthur Boulevard
Mahwah, New Jersey 07430

www.paulistpress.com

Printed and bound in the
United States of America

I dedicate this book to people who face difficulties in relationships, whether in marriage or in their family, at work, or with friendships.

Contents

Introduction ix

Part I: Realities of a Relationship .1
    Chapter 1: Relationships 3
    Chapter 2: The Significant Other 12
    Chapter 3: A Meaningful Relationship 19
    Chapter 4: Inevitable Transitions 25
    Chapter 5: Expectations 35
    Chapter 6: Assumptions and Reality 42
    Chapter 7: Finding Harmony 51
    Chapter 8: Do People Change? 61

Part II: Sensitive Areas 73
    Chapter 9: Facing Disenchantment 75
    Chapter 10: Handling Frustrations 82
    Chapter 11: Anger 88
    Chapter 12: Jealousy 92
    Chapter 13: Other Family Members 96
    Chapter 14: Balancing Work and Relationship 103
    Chapter 15: Managing Money 111

Part III: Sources of Strength 119
    Chapter 16: What Is Love? .121
    Chapter 17: Intimacy 129
    Chapter 18: Choice and Commitment 138
    Chapter 19: Spiritual Strength 146

Epilogue 155

Contents

Appendices 157

   Appendix 1: Human Sexuality 159
   Appendix 2: Tools for Building a Better Marriage 171
   Appendix 3: The Marriage Creed 175

Bibliography 179

Acknowledgments

Living in Difficult Relationships owes its final form and completion to Donna Crilly, managing editor; Paul McMahon, my original editor; and Kathleen Doyle, copy editor. Diligently, Donna and Kathleen went over my manuscript and offered certain valuable suggestions that make this book most effective reading.

I am grateful to:

* The Reverend Father Mark-David Janus, president of Paulist Press, who considered and approved publication of this book.

* The editorial department of Paulist Press for comments and text improvements that made this effort worthwhile. Prior to this work, Paulist Press has published four other books that I have written.

* Pat, my soul mate and supportive wife, whose presence in my life continues to be a real inspiration.

* Margery Hueston and Pattie Menzi, who carefully edited my last draft before I submitted it to the publisher.

* My precious children—Mercene, Michael, Basil, and Katina—and four lovable grandchildren—Nikki, Andrew, Stacey Mercene, and Peter Andrea, who have brought much joy and fun into my life.

* My numberless clients who, over the years, besides receiving my heartfelt counseling, also read and appreciate my writings.

Introduction

There are hundreds of self-help books available, offering suggestions or options that could possibly improve a marriage or any significant relationship. However, this book is different; it moves steadily into the important aspects of life and clarifies the potential within each spouse to make their marriage better. It is based on the belief that a good relationship can be built by any two people who are willing to face the truth about themselves as individuals and who understand the worthiness of living life together. The key issue is to *see and accept* the reality of life with another person, not the fantasy presented by Hollywood shows. If the purpose of marriage is to make people happy, why is it that divorces are a common occurrence? People who find happiness in being together work and cooperate to make their relationship pleasant.

In my years as a marriage and family therapist, I have learned that a good marriage requires carefully informed and willing participants who envision a relationship that provides fulfillment and purpose. The journey through married life is not always smooth. When two people take a calculated risk and decide to travel together because they love each other, inevitably they will encounter challenges and difficulties. The couple needs to face these encounters with mature love, honesty, patience, tolerance, trust, and respect for each other.

A good marriage provides fulfillment, joy, peace, and love in all its fullness. It is a discovery of who we truly are, God's creation. This kind of love is not outside; it is deep within us. We can never lose it, and it cannot leave us. The realization that we are creatures of love with the potential of loving others makes us aware of the good that exists within each of us and gives us knowledge of how this good part can be shared with our partner.

In the process of writing this book, I mentioned the title to several people—friends, relatives, and some professionals in the field of the healing arts—primarily to see their reaction. The responses of most women were unanimous: *I would love to read such a book. My husband is a very difficult man. He expects far too much of me. Other men have fun with their wives and enjoy doing activities together. My husband's idea of fun is watching sports on television on Sunday afternoons.* Men's responses did not vary much: *I should be reading a book about wives who are not easy to live with. Women are hard to please. I don't know what to do to make my wife happy, and I don't think she knows either.* Men think of their wives as being difficult. Women feel that their husbands are difficult. Blaming the other is much easier than admitting that both contribute to their difficulties, but it does not lead to a solution to the situation. The quality of their contributions may be different. In times of marital discord, I wonder how many couples really consider what the better qualities of the relationship are and what effort they make to amplify them. The basic needs of most people who get married or make a commitment to be together are to complete and improve their lives. As you delve into the contents of this book, you may notice the purpose of the chapters is to provide insights and tools to meet these needs.

The fact that you have picked up this book and read thus far shows that you are wondering what, if anything, you can do for your relationship. Do not underestimate yourself. There is a lot you can do. You remember your initial love when you met this particular individual and you said, "*This is the one I would like to marry.*" What about your mutual promises *to honor and cherish till death do us part?*

If you are envisioning the end of the honeymoon and if you are questioning the lifelong sharing and happiness, then you are definitely ready to meet a new challenge. If a serious issue unexpectedly surfaces in your marriage and you are feeling emotionally disconnected from your spouse, and if your self-esteem seems to be crumbling like a stately old building under the blows of the wrecking ball and nothing seems to make sense, then expect the unexpected. Your doubts may strengthen you to face this challenge. There may be a price to pay for such a challenge, but as you face it with courage and faith, you will discover a better self.

Often these feelings of hopelessness occur in what are known as *good marriages*. Frustrations and doubts do not come over us all of a sudden; rather they creep gradually, in stages. Distance increases between husband and wife as they passively watch their relationship wither. Mates look at each other with concern and wonder, *Can this relationship really survive?* Yes it can, when both mates patiently try to apply love as one of the greatest ingredients of our existence, God's gift to all humans. Marriage implies an effort to move from love platitudes to love attitudes—and action. This is your challenge. Your peace of mind and health of body and soul are totally dependent upon a good relationship with your significant other.

PMK

PART I

Realities of a Relationship

CHAPTER I

Relationships

When we love, we ought not to bind others to ourselves with the shackles of our affection.

We do not really love when we inflict upon others the burden of our love.

We ought never to manipulate people so as to mold them to our own way of thinking under the pretext of our love for them.

Louis-Marie Parent

We are born into relationships, and as we grow we experience many different relationships. From the first breath upon birth to our last breath on earth we live, move, and are in one relationship or another. The quality of our relationships is formed and shaped by a family system—often a mother and father whose commitment is to live harmoniously together and to raise healthy and happy children. A child's behavior and emotions are influenced by his parents from infancy through adolescence. Sometimes without realizing it, parents teach values and attitudes. They help to develop children socially and they play a major role in their children's enculturation.

Over the years, single-parent families have increased in number. It is difficult to evaluate the development of a child raised in a single-parent environment. Conceivably, such a child might not only miss the absent parent, but with that role model removed, the enormity of the task for the remaining parent is increased significantly.

Children often emulate parental attitudes and behavior. When both parents respect each other, children learn the principle of respect. If children witness actions of love and forgiveness, they learn to love and forgive; if they witness quarrels and criticism, they learn to quarrel and criticize; if they see parents working together, they learn the importance of teamwork. From this information, it is not hard to understand that when children receive love and support, they are more apt to have successful relationships regardless of economics. There is no guarantee that a child from a rich family will be a better individual than one from a poor family.

The family forms the basis of how we learn to relate to ourselves and with others. In fact, all relationships have their origins in the unique and complex system of a family. For example, a single child growing up in relation to a parent or parents can receive a great deal of attention but miss the interaction with siblings. The arrival of a second or third child provokes intense feelings in the first child and triggers the initial stages of sibling rivalry.

The problem of sibling rivalry and jealousy can be carried into adult life. There are many examples of adults—brothers or sisters—not speaking to one another. Such situations can destroy potentially good relationships and impact a person's habits and lifestyle.

Our ability to function in society depends upon the emotional security and the intellectual capacity we gain in the home. It is in the home that we learn guidelines for behavior and discern directions for the future. As young adults we enter a time of vocational and marital choices—two of the most significant decisions that we confront. As we mature, new thoughts surface and we anticipate answers to such questions as: *Can my goals be achieved and my dreams fulfilled? Do my most significant relationships provide fulfillment and happiness? How do I deal with disappointment and disenchantment?*

Relationships can be good and productive or they can be troubled and destructive. It depends upon how people perceive and respond to each other. This book is written primarily for those who have a difficult relationship and want to identify the underlying problems and find viable solutions.

In our contemporary world, there are a number of factors that contribute to the development of the way we relate as people. Mass media, Hollywood celebrities, and print advertising are strong influences. Essentially, as a son learns to relate to his father, he gradually learns what it means to be a man. Dr. Frank Pittman encapsulates the father-son relationship in one sentence: "*A man learns masculinity primarily from his father.*"

Generations of boys who grow up without caring fathers or male mentors are left to guess what men are really like. They look to cultural icons—larger-than-life images—as role models of masculinity. From his relationship with his mother, a son learns what women are all about and how to relate to them.

Similarly, a daughter learns from her mother how to be a woman. Early in life, a girl imitates her mother, and as she grows older she might even compete with her. *Mom, what you can do, I can do also.* From her father she learns what men are like, and if she happens to have a good relationship with her father, she may look for a mate who has similar characteristics.

With the home influence and programming we receive, as maturity sets in, either we adjust to each new relationship or we walk away from it. The quality of interaction with another human being depends mainly on our self-confidence and self-esteem. What seems to be important is that a relationship based solely on emotions cannot function very effectively. The heart, the center of feelings, cannot maintain a relationship. It is the head that must take the lead. Simply, when head and heart work together, a relationship blossoms. In a romantic encounter, however, when someone says, *I love you. I cannot live without you. You are the person of my dreams,* that person has engaged the heart. Loving someone in his or her preferred manner can be emotionally exhausting.

Some siblings have to struggle to be able to establish fruitful relationships. Two sisters, Doris and Frances, started individual therapy. Both married and had children, but maintained no contact with each other. They celebrated major holidays apart.

Not only did they deprive themselves of a loving exchange, they also forbade their children from interacting with their cousins. Doris divorced; she worked hard as a single parent to maintain her family. Frances had a troubled relationship with her husband, but for practical reasons she decided to stay married. In an outburst of anger, she said, "*As soon as my kids become adults, I'm getting a divorce.*"

Frank and Jerry, two brothers born eighteen months apart, had not spoken to each other for ten years. Their mother's death gave rise to inheritance issues, and that was the cause of their long silence. They refused to have any contact with each other from that point on. Jerry, the younger brother, felt controlled and manipulated by his older brother. Frank claimed that his brother was immature and selfish. "*I'm trying to help him but nothing seems to make him happy. He thinks I'm controlling his life.*"

By his third visit to my office, Frank admitted that his marriage was on the brink of a breakup. In one of our sessions, he spoke about his wife. "She's a beautiful woman but her many interests overwhelm me. She loves shopping, browsing in department stores, visiting museums, and vacationing in foreign countries. Parties delight her; hearing and repeating funny stories make her laugh. She loves to chat with friends over the phone and discuss their latest news and their children's activities. All these things, so desirable to her, I find tedious and boring."

"How do you respond to your wife's interests?" I asked.

"I go along. I tolerate each situation to maintain peace," Frank said.

"Just tolerate?"

"I could be a better husband," he said, "but I feel constrained by her needs, and I ignore my own. One day, I lifted a heavy box and hurt my back. My wife was not sympathetic. 'Don't worry,' she said to me. 'Take an Aleve and you'll feel better. I have to do some shopping.' She pulled the car out of the garage and off she went."

Unable to be in charge of his married life and afraid to lay claim to his needs, Frank found himself continually compromising. He experienced chest pains and his blood pressure soared. Meanwhile, he criticized his brother, saying that he ought to be more involved in his married life.

Jerry was bipolar, and his marriage had become a battle-field. His own ups and downs further distanced him from his wife. He became verbally abusive. He came to the conclusion he had married the wrong woman, and he looked for reasons to let go of his marriage. "We have nothing in common; we are different," he claimed. "We can't have a conversation without getting into an argument."

One day his wife packed up her belongings and moved into her mother's house. Feeling alone and lonely, Jerry asked me, his therapist, to phone his wife. "We can start marriage counseling together," he said. "I don't want her to leave me. I can change." When I phoned his wife, she emphatically said, "Our marriage is over. I should have left him two years ago."

"Could you at least join your husband in my office for a counseling session?"

"I don't think so," she said. "I feel for him, but he's not going to change. Jerry can shred me to pieces in five minutes. He twists what I say and puts words in my mouth. He belittles what I do for him. I can never please him. He's an unhappy man. When something goes wrong in our home, he blames me and accuses me of being inept and then—Doctor, you won't believe what he expects of me. He wants sex."

Both sets of siblings came from different families and had different backgrounds; their marital problems brought them to my office. In speaking individually with the two brothers and the two sisters, I discovered that they were currently involved in sibling rivalry, but their initial struggle was with their own selves. Evidently when they were children, they lacked emotional support. They grew up with a number of dependency needs, and they had still not outgrown their need for emotional and personal support. *This need for nurturing and support is a primary underlying motive for marriage—though people are not always aware of its importance. Ideally, all of us want a partner who is accepting, loving, understanding, protective, and genuinely caring. On the flip side, lack of emotional support is a frequent cause of dissatisfaction within a relationship.* Their love for each other, instead of being based on the love that they had within themselves, was based on their exterior attitudes and on their behavior. Strangely enough, individually each of them reacted with a similar proclamation: *I do love my sister. I love my brother, but....*

Underlying their individual therapy lay the hope that they would learn to look more deeply *within* in order to discover the potential for a loving relationship. If we are willing to accept our own humanness, our good points and our imperfections, then it is easier to accept brothers, sisters, and spouses. Acceptance of another person involves consent on our part to leave them as they are without expecting them to change for us. Acceptance, however, does not imply the compromise of our own principles in order to accommodate the ideologies of another person. It presupposes strength of character and a way of life that is but an echo and a reflection of our conscience, of our "inner being."

Acceptance as a spiritual concept and practice may be a powerful answer to happiness in any relationship, regardless of whether we are married or single. This kind of acceptance has a component of peace.

No matter how much two people have in common—race, ethnic background, family values, religion, politics, financial status—when they enter into a relationship they soon discover the many ways they are different from one another. Everyone knows that, but most of us don't know how to deal with the differences; instead, we are often frightened or threatened by them. We use them to belittle one another and battle in endless power struggles. Frequently we damage or destroy what might otherwise be a very good relationship.

There are occasions when relationships precipitate psychological discomforts that can affect us physically with migraine headaches, backaches, and arthritis, even ulcers. This was the case with Debby, an attractive forty-year-old widow. Her husband had had cancer and had died three years ago. She sat silently in my office, not knowing how to start. Eyes and face gave the impression that she was still in mourning. I thought she was going to tell me about the loss of her husband.

"How can I help you?" I asked.

"My relationship with my second husband is making me sick. I feel crushed and demolished."

"What seems to be the problem?"

"I married George eighteen months ago. I didn't want to spend the rest of my life alone. Loneliness is terrible." She sighed. When I met him through a friend, he seemed generous and caring. He was a handsome man, fun to be with. Instantly, I had good feelings for him, but..." she paused.

"But...what?"

"My first husband was an angel. He loved me; he would do anything for me; he made me laugh and appreciated every little thing I did for him. But the Lord decided to take him. Three years later, I married George. I'm very unhappy. I never had any physical problems, and now I'm going from doctor to doctor— daily migraines and upset stomach. George says he loves me, but he argues with me from morning till night. If I say it's a beautiful day, he says what's beautiful about it? He always finds something wrong with me. He complains about my cooking, the way I keep house, my hairstyle, and the amount of money I spend on my clothes.

"I confided my situation to my mother and she advised me to divorce him." After a few seconds of thought, Debby said, "Doctor, I don't believe in divorce. But I'm concerned about my health."

In subsequent sessions we talked about her life, both the happy and unhappy experiences. By her sixth session she became aware of some positive aspects of her personality. She decided to speak calmly to her husband, even if it meant broaching the subject several times. In view of her husband's attitude, she tried to explain without acrimony her actual feelings and how she visualized her relationship with him. She asked him to join her in marital therapy. Debby wanted, at all costs, to regain the confidence of her companion and to believe in his rare declaration of love. After four joint sessions of marital therapy, George began to see Debby not as an enemy to be defeated but as a human being, a loving companion who could love him and who deserved his respect. Until the present writing, both are still in therapy. Their progress indicates that their love for each other is far deeper than they are willing to admit.

Can love succeed based on the differences between two people instead of on their commonalities? If love is mature and unselfish, Yes! In fact, the only way we truly feel loved is through the trust we build knowing that our partner loves us for the real person that we are, distinctly different from him or her. With a simple change in perspective, those very same differences can become doorways to the deepest intimacy and the sweetest spiritual meaning a relationship can offer.

You can transform differences into catalysts for change, personal growth, and ongoing adventures instead of recipes for disaster and heartache. When you shift your perspective, your partner's opinions, feelings, and behaviors are no longer *wrong or ridiculous*. They are just different. Your partner's values are important just as your values are.

The spiritual richness of your relationship can unfold as you both become sincerely curious about each other. You no longer assume you already know what each other thinks and you do not take each other's moods for granted. Instead, if you value your relationship, you must stay open to learning more about who your partner is, through and through. Then each of you will become more connected, more present, awake, and alive. And that is the objective of this book: to help the reader realize that by recognizing his or her potential he or she can live effectively in a difficult relationship.

As I bring this chapter to a close, I will indulge in a personal fantasy: It is my wish that someday soon our world will be different. That spouses, people living together, significant others, friends, and siblings will accept each other as being different, learn to respect each other, and live harmoniously. That mothers and fathers, biological or adoptive, will raise children from birth to adulthood by being responsible, happy, healthy, attentive, loving, and ethical role models. Then we will need far fewer police officers and fewer prisons; we will have fewer wars and far fewer books on how to live happily in a given relationship. We wage battles within our society, but the real battlefield for a better world in a free society lies within caring, genuine, and loving relationships.

THOUGHTS TO CONSIDER:

- Relationships are fragile. Though difficult people come in every shape and size and in either gender, each wrestles with similar issues because the goals are the same: control and win, regardless of what it takes. People use weapons of emotional destruction such as anger, criticism, denial, guilt, rejection, and withdrawal to survive in difficult relationships.

- Turning a toxic relationship into a healthy one requires hard work and a new vision. You cannot change your situation if you fail to see the problems and the options. Objectivity in healthy relationships encourages each person to be responsible for his or her own choices and actions and the consequences of them.

- Respecting differences is crucial to getting along with people. You could share stories of people you cherish, even admire, who think, act, react, and choose differently than you. Perhaps you seek advice from those who offer different perspectives. You laugh with people who you believe are *out to lunch or who do not have all their oars in the water*. Like meals, people and relationships would be boring if they were all the same.

- Perhaps you are hoping and waiting for that difficult person in your life to start doing things differently. Maybe you believe that if your difficult person changes, he or she will not be so offensive to you, will be more fun to be with and, therefore, be more likeable. Maybe you are right, but your expectations may be unrealistic. Basically, people do not change. The hope is that they will mature and behave humanly.

- A healthy relationship implies a give-and-take interaction. However, there must be limits. It cannot be all give on one side and all take on the other. In handling conflict, your part is not to get pushed back into a reactive and defensive position, regardless of what your difficult person says or does. Love is what holds hearts together when minds disagree.

CHAPTER 2

The Significant Other

Marriage is one of the most complex yet lasting institutions ever established by humans. Challenges, problems and surprises are ever present in every intimate relationship. These require tolerance, compromise, and genuine effort, when a couple cares very deeply about the quality of their relationship and wishes to improve that quality to its best potential.

Mel Krantzler

As you ponder the chapters of this book, I suggest that you take the time to look deeply into your self and your life. Find a quiet place, relax, and think attentively. Gently explore aspects of your married life that currently are disturbing and visualize possibilities of improvement. A periodic, personal inventory and reevaluation of your relationship are necessary for a happier life.

Deep down in the human heart lies a strong longing to love and be loved. Choosing a person to be in love with and with whom you wish to share your life is a wonderful experience. You surely remember the sensation that shook you from head to toe when you discovered that particular person; you felt excited, complete, and you said to yourself, *There is nothing else I want. My dream has come true! Here is someone I can talk with and someone who understands me and accepts me without harsh criticisms or judgments. In this one's loving presence I can be myself: honest, genuine, and real. Truly, this is the person I want to be with for the rest of my life.* You were in a state of ecstasy!

Many couples who find themselves in this state of exuberance, *being in love*, make a decision to be together for life. In reality, does any couple have a guarantee that their marriage will last till death do us part? Most people enter married life with love and faith, and the expectation that their relationship will be perfect. Let's not delude ourselves. Good relationships do not come easily; they are a result of hard work. Each spouse must be willing to work on the marriage, be skillful in ways to resolve problems, and be strong in the commitment to succeed. In critical times, spouses need to have strength and sensitivity and be able to look into each other's eyes and say, *I love you*, and mean it.

Initially, most couples are in constant motion; they visit friends and go away for weekends, celebrating life as if there were no tomorrow. Each mate tends to the gratification of the other with a sort of illusive indulgence. There is an abundance of enthusiasm and energy in their activities. There are no obstacles, and each performs tasks with a great deal of patience and understanding. There is nothing that one will not do for the other, no mistake for which one will not forgive the other, and no errand that one will not run for the other.

A permeating dream with couples in love continues to be the hope that their relationship will be better than any other marriage they have observed, including that of their parents. The truth is that it *can* be better—but not without hard work and responsibility. The ability to respond to each other's needs is an essential ingredient for a successful marriage. In a loving relationship, flexibility is much easier to practice than it is in an unstable relationship.

The daily structure of a couple without children allows for a wide variety of solutions to immediate problems. For example, either or both partners may prepare dinner; they may choose to go out to a restaurant; they may drop in at a friend's or visit their parents' house for a meal; or they may eat separately. The birth of children changes the climate, even among the most loving of couples; the arrival of a child marks the beginning of a critical time of transition. The physical and emotional presence of a child usually changes the marital interaction. The distribution of duties, the division of domestic responsibilities—who will shop, cook, pick up the child at the child-care center, wash dishes, and do laundry—have to be clearly defined. At this point, great care must be taken to ensure that husband and wife do not become rigid or inflexible. Perhaps you have already traveled this road and all of the above sounds familiar. At this juncture of your life, then, what caused the change in the situation?

As you may recall, early in your married life you probably applied patterns of behavior that were mutually satisfying. In every way, you tried to impress and please your partner. However, each of you came from a different family and brought into your marriage individual behaviors—different expectations, rules, and values—and yet you anticipated the development of a happy lifestyle. You may have thought it would be an easy transition from single to married life. Perhaps it was an improved and revised version of your parents' style that you brought to your marriage. Eventually you developed a marital coalition that provided fulfillment for your physical and esthetic needs and encouraged emotional involvement and cooperation with your spouse. Each of you appropriated time to discuss issues, negotiate, renegotiate, and compromise to resolve conflicts. In time, as you lived together, you discovered viable solutions to personal issues, from deciding when to eat to deciding when to make love. Together you decided what was worth fighting over and when to make up. These are details of married life with which most couples are familiar.

Most of us enter married life in a romantic state. We want our relationship to be the way we envision it—we want it our way. We ignore the fact that we bring someone else into our life who has his or her own ideas of how the marriage should be designed. When we do not get our own way, the result is a troubled marriage. If the relationship is to survive, both spouses have to understand the adaptation theory: that is, marriage requires ongoing adjustment; it demands a continuous give and take to enable each experience to be loving and rewarding to each partner. No marriage is problem-free. In good marriages, couples solve their problems constructively instead of wallowing in the belief that the grass is greener in other couples' gardens.

Of course there are matters that cannot change in the marriage package. For example, if you do not like certain attitudes of your in-laws, you cannot do much to persuade them to change to your way of thinking. Nor can you punish your spouse because of your unhappiness with your in-laws. Together, you establish boundaries so your life together can grow and develop to meet your needs and the needs of your relationship. You do not need external sources—parents, relatives, or friends—to tell you how you should run your married life. Love and respect your in-laws, relatives, and friends, but safeguard what you have built and are still building together as a couple. It is of no benefit to tell the other, *You are just like your mother,* or *You are just like your father,* or to insult relatives with nasty words.

If wisdom comes after a particular crisis, then you can evaluate an existing disagreement and develop it into a growth experience. *Why is it that I want to win this argument?* you may ask yourself. In every Garden of Eden there is a snake—in every marriage there is imperfection, for spouses are imperfect human beings. When the snake is still a worm, dispose of it before it becomes a monster. As soon as a conflict begins, try to solve it immediately by discussion and negotiation. Every problem has an answer. Give your answer. Listen to your mate's answer, respect it as you respect your own, and combine both answers to solve the problem. This is your contribution to the initiation of good communications in your married life.

Already you know that as you live and share life together, other sets of issues surface, and realistic responses need to be found. Issues include deciding how to celebrate holidays, planning vacations, visiting your in-laws, maintaining friends and socializing, giving presents, spending money, purchasing personal and household items, doing domestic chores, organizing house improvements, and belonging to a community. Like a growing child whose needs change from year to year, *you change physically, mentally, and spiritually,* and your married life also changes; it matures, and a constant emergence of needs have to be faced realistically. In time, ramifications of married life cause anxiety, frustration, and impasses that seem hard to transcend. By this time, you have probably overcome some major obstacles and feel at peace with your resolution. Currently, though, something is happening to your inner self, and your mind is seeking relief. You may think you have made a terrible mistake by marrying and you feel like running away. Many people do run; others face the challenge and give their marriage another chance.

Conceivably, with the transition from single life to the more mature married life, marital coexistence challenged you and caused anxiety, even in the early years. Deep down in your heart, you did not want to end a relationship that started with love and a promise. You may have reached the point at which you are saying to yourself repeatedly, *Guess this is it. I have had it and can't stand it much longer. It's not worthwhile continuing this marriage.* Take another look into your marriage. In the middle of your crisis, when an impulse darts across your mind and says, *Walk out. Just get up and leave. Run away.* Do not act rashly; pause and pull back. Take three deep breaths, offer a prayer to God for guidance, and rehearse the response you owe your partner: *I love you. I will always love you, and I will find a way to make things work for us.*

At this very moment, stand in front of a mirror and look at yourself. Why are you holding this book? Perhaps an invisible power, the best part within you, your spiritual self, guided you to buy it. If you believe this thought, take another deep breath, relax, and start reading slowly. Life is still ahead of you. Let the above inventory and the chapters that follow provide you with sensible thoughts to consider. You may discover something about yourself; it may be your own ability to remodel your inner space. Stay with this reading for a week.

There is a rich life in front of you today, but it needs to be cultivated. Instead of looking outside for fulfillment or pleasure, for validation, security, or love, you have a treasure within that is infinitely greater than anything the world can offer. Avoid a power struggle and refrain from trying to change the other. Say to yourself, *I married this person because I loved him or her. I know my partner can be lovable. I am discovering unloving blemishes in my spouse; I have blemishes also. My mate is not perfect and neither am I. Some aspects of our life together need to change. We must make the changes together in order to maintain harmony in our being together and to make our efforts productive.*

Before you start reading the next chapter, take time out, sit comfortably, go over this chapter once more, and possibly reread parts you may have underlined with your spouse.

THOUGHTS TO CONSIDER:

1. Can any spouse really fulfill all the needs of the other? Why not?

   There is not a human being that walks on this planet that can totally satisfy all the needs of someone else.

2. Love can make many things happen. Can love solve all the problems that arise in married life?

   Love cannot put a roof over our heads, pay the mortgage or the rent of a home, put food on the table or buy clothes or pay taxes. All these existential needs are being met because spouses love each other and care enough to be responsible citizens.

3. There must have been other people in your life. Why is it that you have chosen this particular person?

   The signs for a promising relationship seemed to be present with this person. In our interaction while dating, I sensed good intentions, solidarity, and moral integrity—characteristics of a good human being.

4. Are you aware that all your expectations have not been met? Are you able to articulate them to your partner in a nondefensive way?

   Yes, many of my expectations have not been met—mainly because they are unrealistic. If I cannot fulfill these expectations myself, I don't bother discussing them with my spouse. But when I sense that my expectations are reasonable, I make them known in a gentle manner. Being defensive or persistent evokes anger in the other and accomplishes nothing.

5. What are you personally able and willing to contribute to turn your relationship around and make your being together a more rewarding experience?

   Instead of always seeking my own satisfaction, I look into the eyes of the person I have chosen to be with the rest of my life and ask myself, What else can I do to make our relationship rewarding?

6. If your marriage has been turbulent for a long time, would you be willing to take time out to reassess your situation and even consult a marriage therapist?

    That is a desirable and wise direction to take. When I notice that our disagreements become conflicts that we don't seem able to resolve, I take a positive attitude and try to present to my spouse the possibility of consulting a marriage therapist. When facing serious issues, I believe external help is needed.

7. You are endowed with a body and soul. You also have a functional mind. These are irreplaceable gifts. Are you willing to use these constructively in connection with your spouse?

    A dialogue with my spouse seems to be of great benefit. When we are both relaxed, I carefully share ideas or plans—one idea or plan at a time, lest I overwhelm my spouse.

8. Saying *I love you* and meaning it is a blessing. Making a conscious commitment to be lovable requires effort and honesty. Can you be loving and lovable to your spouse?

    It is not always easy; sometimes I do not feel loving or my spouse is not lovable. I know I am capable of loving, but I also need to be lovable.

9. Marital harmony is the fruit of joint participation: creative cooperation of two people who recognize the importance of caring and being respectful. Are you able to take a serious look at your spouse and say, *I care?*

    Yes, I care. Otherwise, I would not be reading this book. Deep down, I am a caring person. I care for my well-being and the wellness of my marriage.

10. To keep a marriage happy takes goodwill and genuine effort. Can you turn to your partner and say, *Let's try to improve the state of our marriage. You and I are intelligent people, and we surely must be able to make our marriage better?*

    This is truly the challenge in every marriage. Good marriages can become better when each spouse takes time to consider the value of married life.

CHAPTER 3

A Meaningful Relationship

> The mystery of a significant relationship is part of the mystery of the person: it is an aspect of the universal challenge every man and woman face as soon they become free to think and to act on their own.
>
> José de Vinck

A good marriage begins with a man and a woman who form a loving, psychologically sound relationship that provides stability, financial security, and material benefits. A serious relationship consists of personal needs, attitudes, ambitions, expectations, and issues that require solutions. Emphasis is placed on what one partner does and how the other responds. Feelings and attitudes, both conscious and unconscious, are gradually revealed, and reciprocal attention must be paid so they do not become obstacles in the relationship. The purpose of reciprocity is to bring emotional stability and happiness to both partners. The degree of satisfaction that each spouse derives from the other and the relationship depends on how well expectations are met.

During the early stages of married life, issues set the mood for adjustment. For example, it does not take long to become aware that one likes the bedroom window closed and the other likes it open. How partners compromise each situation is what is vital. A married person who insists on living the lifestyle of a single person and keeps the window open or closed without regard for the partner's preference is doomed to an unhappy relationship. Sooner or later, hurt and anger build up in the partner.

This eventually causes an angry reaction from the one who wants to continue the behavior of a single person and expects the partner to *do it my way*. Such behavior is added to the list of frustrations or resentments.

A simple disagreement like the one described can trigger a negative pattern of interaction between spouses that will surface in other areas of living. Certainly it cannot create a loving relationship that both can enjoy. The one who is able to be flexible, perhaps opening the window halfway to please the other, is paving the way for better communication. It is not that the flexible one is giving in or giving up; rather, it is a partner seeking common satisfactory ground. If there is failure to show appreciation for the compromise, the flexible spouse may at least gain satisfaction in thinking, *After all, I did the right thing!*

There is a tendency to hope for magical personality changes in one another after marriage. It is more realistic to believe in the possibility of personality growth. Such growth should continue throughout a person's life through psychological awareness and adjustments that enable him or her to fulfill their potential. The knowledge of this potential for growth should give hope to troubled husbands and wives who visualize a better marriage.

When their relationship became intimate and thoughts about marriage were openly discussed, Linda felt increasing anxiety against Greg's smoking. Looking at the rainbow of romance, she thought that when they got married Greg would quit his bad habit. During their honeymoon, although still unhappy about his smoking, Linda said nothing. When a dear friend asked her how she enjoyed her honeymoon, she said with a smile, "*Wonderful! Greg is a great guy. He's the man of my dreams. But when I kiss him, it feels as if I were putting my nose in an ashtray.*"

In the third month of their marriage, Linda finally decided it was time to take a firm stand on the topic of Greg's smoking. She was sensitive in her approach to the subject, for she was aware he was addicted. Although his father had died of lung cancer, apparently Greg did not believe such a disease would attack him, so he was not willing to deny himself what he called *one of the pleasures in his life.* Linda pointed out to him the damaging effect his smoking could have on their health and the health of their future children. Eventually Greg was persuaded to think seriously about quitting. After many discussions, one day Greg looked into Linda's teary eyes and said, "*Our marriage is important to me and so is our health, and, therefore, I'm going to do something about my demon. Just be patient with me.*" He invested time and money in a program that helped him to give up smoking. Three years later, Linda and Greg and their twin girls are enjoying a healthy family life. While the personalities of the couple may not have changed dramatically, their relationship has become more mature and happier. As their story indicates, when we tackle issues in a spirit of respect and humility we can achieve positive results; it is likely that such results could not have been achieved if they had approached each other in an attitude of hostility.

In troubled marriages, it is natural to observe only the negative aspects of a partner or of the marriage itself and give little or no consideration to the positive aspects. Often I ask troubled couples to describe at least one positive aspect of their marriage. After they have told me all the wrongs *and all the evils have emerged from their Pandora's box*, I pause and wait. If they mention one good thing—*we still love each other*—there is hope. Something good remains. When a husband and wife become aware of the good possibilities that exist in their marriage, they can be helped to recognize the direction it should take. Husbands and wives can be led to greater awareness and acceptance of their own limitations as well as those of their spouses; when they reach that point, they can formulate new and reasonable marital goals.

In good marriages interaction is constructive, enabling each partner to live life more fully. Each partner should be independent and should be able, if necessary, to walk the road of life alone, but each should feel that together they would be able to live a fuller life.

A husband and wife are a team, self-accepting and respecting the other's uniqueness. Neither partner should withhold, waiting for the other to give. Rather, each should give freely to the other because of the satisfaction and pleasure derived from doing so. A good marriage requires mature people who are willing to commit themselves to *common life* goals. They *may* marry in order to *give* to the other, not merely for what they may *get*, not simply to attain happiness, but to achieve a strong, gratifying, interdependent relationship. There should be give and take in marriage, and taking should be secondary to giving.

A top priority is the sharing of responsibility in determining mutual marital goals. Intelligence, accountability, shared information, and insight give a relationship a sense of direction. Self-acceptance and mutual tolerance help spouses to communicate with minimal frustration and friction. If anger does arise, it is important to express it at the appropriate time in an appropriate manner. Trying to put the other down, trying to win, trying to have one's way are losing strategies. Tearing the other down in the presence of others is destructive. Many people make unrealistic demands of themselves, their partner, or their marriage. Unable to fulfill these demands, they criticize themselves severely, using a standard of perfection, a standard incompatible with man's nature. Normal standards of judgment do not require perfection.

When we focus on our spouse's weaknesses, contempt and resentment influence our reaction. Every human being, every spouse, has strong and weak points. If we want to find them, without a doubt we will. If we want to obsess about the weaknesses, they will grow and become magnified in our minds.

Couples must use their minds to the fullest extent but in a spirit of humility. They may exert their total energies to attain their agreed marital goals. This does not mean that a husband or wife is all-wise, omniscient, omnipotent, and infallible.

Sometimes, after having thought about an issue as carefully as they could, they realize that an error in judgment has been made, resulting in harmful consequences. Conceivably, they feel disappointed, upset, or guilty, believing that they should have avoided the error, although they do not know what they could have done differently. Errors in judgments or major mistakes do cause setbacks. However, errors often teach the best lessons. It is important that the couple does not wallow in regrets about events that have already taken place. The task is to join efforts and move on with life and living. Mature couples have their own private sanctuary where private issues, problems, and intimacies are discussed alone, peacefully, with a great deal of care and sensitivity.

People who seek fulfillment in marriage may consider the following transition of married life. The human mind is constantly moving, drawn forward by a belief and conviction that better things lie beyond the horizon. We are born and raised in a family and culture that become familiar. At some point, driven by an irresistible attraction of the intimate other, we let go of the familiar and enter the unfamiliar ground of a marriage. Our life suddenly changes, and it will never be the same again: we get married. The quality of any marriage is determined by how both spouses react in letting go of the familiar and adopting a new lifestyle. Both should have adequately resolved issues from earlier years—the family life they have left behind—and realize that a different life lies ahead. They each bring into their life a new person whom they have to respect and consider as Number One.

THOUGHTS TO CONSIDER:

- Perfection does not exist, even in the best relationships. Failings or mistakes often help us to understand human nature or become our stepping-stones to higher attainments. Husbands and wives should fundamentally be committed to each other and patiently develop their relationship.

- Occasional thoughts about having married the wrong person, or fantasies about escaping the bonds of marriage, or entertaining the possibility of another relationship may occur. Troubled spouses may indulge in such possibilities. Problems or incompatibility stifles possibilities of growth. Then the question is: *Does termination of a marriage for whatever reasons guarantee you will find a better relationship?*

- If your goal is to have a better marriage, you have to learn coping strategies to face each obstacle or transition with reasonable success. When you choose to accept changes, you need to consider and explore the unlived potentials within your marriage. What might be an interesting contribution that would make the relationship rewarding? As desirable or difficult as transitions may be, they clear the ground for new growth. They drop the curtain so that the stage can be set for a new scene.

- A good marriage requires maturity on the part of the spouses. Maturity means having the ability to assume responsibility for conditions and problems that arise during life with a partner. Maturity means ability to cope with problems and face life creatively within the reality of one's own marriage.

- Mature couples try to develop increased awareness of each other's needs as they face the various challenges of married life. Each challenge may enhance or hamper life; it may bring pleasure or pain, but it promises growth. Appreciation for every aspect of life requires maturity, sensitivity, responsible action, and consideration of each other's feelings.

CHAPTER 4

Inevitable Transitions

"Who are you?" said the Caterpillar.
"I—I hardly know, Sir, just at present," Alice replied shyly. "At least I know who I *was* when I got up this morning, but I think I must have been changed several times since then."
          Lewis Carroll, *Alice's Adventures in Wonderland*

We are like Alice in her wonderland in that in our lifetime we experience many real changes—physical, mental, intellectual, and spiritual. Some of these changes are difficult to cope with and cause pain, others are welcome and prove to be of great benefit for our growth as mature adults. Of course not all changes affect us deeply, but as we make a transition from one state to another and make a new beginning, we find ourselves stronger, more knowledgeable, and more aware of who we truly are.

Although there is no way to tell us what a particular change means, there are ways of maximizing our chances of finding that meaning. When changes occur in lifestyle—relocating, buying a house, changing jobs, or losing a job—the spouses need to seek a viable solution together. When there is a difference of opinion, spouses need to be careful not to engage in a power struggle—*I'm right and you're wrong. I told you so.* If one wants to be the winner, then the other becomes the loser. The result of a power struggle is emotional distance between the couple. Decisions made because of panic or compulsivity can only cause anxiety. Whatever changes an individual might go through, such changes also apply to the world of married life. Since our interest is in focusing on ways that will make healthier and happier marital relationships, it is important to consider the stages of married life.

1. Courtship • Marriage. Courtship—the time of ecstatic paralysis—has been cleverly designed by God to lure members of the species into reproducing themselves. "...*male and female [God] created them. God blessed them and...said to them: 'Be fruitful and multiply, and fill the earth and have dominion over it'*" (Gen 1:27).

During courtship, individuals lose most of their good judgment. The man and the woman are in a trance. By God's design for procreation or by the magic of nature, they become wonderfully attractive to each other. They find themselves in a state of ecstasy, from the Greek word *ekstasis* meaning *deranged—defined as "the state of being beside oneself, a state of being beyond all reason and self-control."* Individuals in love are in such a dizzy state that they do not think about the reality of married life. Potential problems, issues of responsibility, and the frightful divorce statistics mean nothing to them; it seems obvious that bad marriages are for others only. *Nothing like that can happen to us,* they think. Sometimes the betrothed partners know they are marrying the wrong persons, but they are in such romantic passion and are being driven by such loud applause of others that they cannot help themselves. When romance subsides and reality sets in, hard work is required, and each spouse needs to be responsible for the emerging needs of the married life.

2. Nesting. Marriage is the only social unit in which so many changes have to be accommodated in a short time. Some of these changes include ambition, new ideas, risks, decisions, positive actions, and adjustment. There is a positive side to this period of change. Practicing patience, moderation, choosing priorities, and harmonizing multiple experiences—all of these foster growth. The young spouses eventually stabilize themselves emotionally, professionally, and financially, and prepare for the future, for home life, and for procreation. They find a reasonably comfortable residence, be it an apartment or a house, and they furnish and decorate it according to their tastes and financial abilities. They build their nest warm enough for the arrival of babies. Much personal meaning can be derived when the couple is planning to have a child. The anticipation of child-bearing and the preparation to accommodate a newborn in their lives necessitate for each spouse considerable personal adjustment. If the relationship is turbulent, having a child would probably cause additional stress.

3. Birth. Young parents combine their efforts to meet the needs of their infant. The focal point is the child and its well-being. At times, the child consumes the mother's energy and the husband feels ignored. On her part, the wife seems to lose interest in her appearance; for months, she does not look after her hair; she doesn't bother to buy new clothes; she doesn't feel attractive. Although she finds fulfillment in caring for her infant, she is overwhelmed physically and mentally by the demands of mother-hood.

For some mothers it takes a long time to transcend the postpartum depression and readjust to the new experience. This is a sensitive area. Few men understand the agony of conception, pregnancy, and the birthing process. Some men, noticing their wife's emotional involvement in a new love, feel neglected and get the impression that they no longer count. They feel that they are merely providers. During this time, the wise wife needs to make sure to pay attention to her husband, showing concern and affection for him. *You come first in my life. Our baby is important to both of us.* She involves the husband in the baby's life, making him aware that this is his baby as well as hers. Smart husbands get involved in caring and showing interest in the child's growth. This is the time that the family lays strong foundations and sound principles for its future wellness and happiness.

4. Raising the Child. The busy years rearing children and providing for their physical, emotional, psychological, and moral needs present many individual and mutual adjustment problems to couples. Even in critical times, when there is illness or a setback in a young child's daily routine, once the baby's needs are comfortably met or the baby is asleep, it is of benefit for a couple to spend time together to replenish their energy and to catch up on each other's personal needs. Parents should enable each other to find satisfaction in their new relationship with their children and should support each other in the parent-child connection—usually loaded with psychological difficulties. Parents need to be careful that they do not use their children to satisfy their own needs. Is it possible for any parent to be completely satisfied with his or her child? Imagine that as you are watching television you see the following advertisement: *If you are completely satisfied with your children, give us a call: 800-888-0000.* The demands of growing children are exhausting.

Let's hear the order of words first spoken by a child. Probably the first word is *Mama*, and shortly after that we hear *Dada*. The third word may be *more*. These key words represent our deepest human needs—first love, followed by security, and then for *more*—of everything. Parents have to adjust and accommodate their child's increasing needs in a creative and supportive manner, but never at the risk of their own happiness. Showing consideration and support for the other promotes intimacy. This *sharing* of concern and interest in their life together is exceedingly rewarding and leads toward further mutual growth and gratification.

5. School Days. Although parents welcome their child's growth and the start of school, school days require another adjustment. Teachers are, in many ways, extensions of parents. A child is thrust into a stranger's hands, and parents are concerned about the treatment the child will receive. Parents get involved in parent-teacher activities and academic concerns, they show interest in their child's learning and express their appreciation to sensitive teachers. This is an area of great importance that benefits the child and the family.

Granted that today, both husband and wife need to work to meet financial obligations. At the same time, they realize that family growth needs concerted nurturing from both spouses. Working parents who invest time and energy in their occupations may find themselves less involved in familial activities. This does not mean that working parents are less interested in their children than mothers or fathers who can afford to stay at home with their children. Spouses should not neglet each other because of growing children and growing financial demands. If harmony and peace are expected in a family, work and career should not be the most important things in life for either husband or wife.

6. The Turbulent Years of Adolescence. Parents become apprehensive about their child's evolution. Physical, emotional, and spiritual changes take place, accelerated by the current culture and peer pressure. The little girl becomes a woman. She is eager to develop and possibly look like her mom or a television star. The little boy feels the changes and is eager to look and act like an adult.

At best, the parents may pull back and take a look at their growing children, admiring and encouraging them to do what seems appropriate and supporting them in ways that benefit their growth. Overindulging them with goods and unconditional freedom precipitates a difficult future. More-than-generous gifts and abundant financial support is needed, but a better contribution to the child's growth and well-being would be the parents' modeling of a cooperative and loving interaction between them.

7. Adulthood and Adjustment to Society. Often intense feelings of loss occur at this juncture. Parents enjoy the growth of their children. Naturally they miss them when they leave home to start their own lives. They feel proud and fulfilled as their children adjust to society, get lucrative jobs or assume promising positions in the adult world, and achieve relative happiness. Some parents become anxious or disappointed when they notice in their sons' or daughters' lack of motivation or inability to pursue better lifestyles. They see and admire other young people who are seemingly successful, and they wonder what's wrong with their children. Most people are aware of the familiar concept: *Success, wealth, and fame attract attention. Poverty implies deprivation of the goods that life offers.* In reality who can possibly know what is hidden in the human psyche? Parents have difficulty in accepting some realities: they no longer have control over their adult children. Their adult children are constantly challenged to get better jobs and make more money. Like any other human beings, young adults have choices to design and redesign their lives according to their emerging needs. Parents need to accept the decisions of their adult children, although they may disagree with them. A major decision in life is marriage. Parents may agree or disagree over their adult child's choice of a spouse. This is the person your child chose for a lifetime companion. The ultimate bliss for parents should be to see that their children are healthy and happily married.

8. Marriage of Young Adults and Adjustment. Initially, the newly-weds accept their in-laws with excitement and joy. Of course, in-laws need and wish to be accepted by the young couple as loving parents and friends. As time passes and the spouses want to develop a loving and productive relationship, they need to have boundaries. Even with the best of intentions in mind, when in-laws cross boundaries they may be perceived as invaders. It is important for both sets of in-laws to respect their married children and allow them to develop a life of their own. There is a whole chapter in this book entitled "Other Family Members" that you may consider.

Usually spouses hope and wish to develop a *loving mindset* that can be a cementing force to keep the marriage intact. Genuine love is most important in marriage, but few spouses are prepared for it, or capable of experiencing it right after the wedding. It comes as a result of a good attitude and years of hard work and patience.

9. The Nest Is Empty. When spouses reach the empty-nest period, they need each other's support. They evaluate their respective careers and style of life and make decisions about *a change or readjustment* that would enhance the marital bond. It tends to be a critical time for spouses who have invested many years of full involvement and concern with their children's growth, education, and establishment in the adult world. During this time other concerns surface. When the adult children move out of the house to make their own lives, spouses look at each other in wonder. *What are we left with, except the sheer habit of living together?* The empty nest becomes an unbearable situation because, as the parents look at each other, they often realize that they cannot maintain a worthwhile dialogue. The only positive direction that remains to be explored is a new *intimacy*. This *empty-nest* period offers much potential for further growth, depending on the relationship that has been built. Both parents miss their children of course, but they should be equipped to accept the forward movement of life with its inevitable changes. It is an important transition. Whatever has taken place is over; it cannot be brought back. Hopefully, it was good for each spouse's individual growth. Now the focus may be on the relationship of the older couple once again. For example, men may wish to encourage their wives to pursue desired careers or to participate more intensely in educational, community, or social activities. Personal inventory often reveals that both men and women in the older age bracket are valuable resources. This is *harvest time*, a time to enjoy the fruits of one's labors.

Wives may encourage their husbands to pursue hobbies and community activities. They may wish to encourage their husbands to embark on a new career that previously they had been reluctant to attempt. It is important that neither feels threatened by the other's interests. Each may help the other to adjust to the changes that are taking place in their lives. This may be a period of increased intimacy. The love and affection that were invested in children can be reinvested in each other in a mature and realistic manner.

10. Middle Age. Menopause in the woman and climacteric in the man occur. In both situations deep feelings of loss of femininity and masculinity are experienced.

There is a kind of middle-age mystique that assumes we have it made by this time, so we may have to settle down and sail tranquilly on without too many storms. This *middlescence*, as it is called, is often adolescence in reverse. During our adolescent years we were asking such questions as: *What can I become? What is worth fighting for? Who are my friends? Who are my enemies? Who could I marry that would make me happy?* In middlescence, we are asking: *What am I doing here? I hate the way my life has turned out. What do I really want? I have no clue. Would I like to do something for the public good or try my hand at artistic ventures or become involved in*

31

nature study? Maybe I should remodel my house or sell it and live in a condominium. Parents in the middle years begin to feel the inevitable aging process, and sometimes their own ailing parents need care, and that causes fear of the ultimate reality of death.

During this time some spouses stray, seeking excitement in another relationship. Often, if their escapades become known, friends and relatives explain it as *middle-age crisis.* Many divorces occur during these years when spouses visualize a more exciting life with someone else: *a woman who will understand all my needs— a man who will take me to places and make me laugh.* No woman and no man in this world could totally satisfy the insatiable needs of the partner.

11. Grandparenthood. Married children become parents themselves, and the additional new role of grandparent, full of pleasures and pitfalls, is assumed. Grandparenthood, as desirable a state of life as it may appear to be, needs to be faced responsibly. If boredom or a feeling that *there's nothing much left in our relationship* dominates, the advent of a grandchild may seem like an opportunity to fill that void with love and affection. Nurturing and caring for the infant make grandparents feel needed and wanted. If grandparents wish to devote most of their time to babysitting, the young parents may be only too happy to grant their wish. But there is another reality: if the grandparents become too involved with their grandchildren, the grown-up children may resent their ongoing presence, because young couples consider the parenting function as their own prideful responsibility. As a strong couple, the grandparents need to find a healthy balance between nurturing their grandchildren and nurturing their own marriage.

12. The Death of a Spouse. Everything that lives eventually dies. Dying begins at the moment of birth. Spouses have to face the inevitability of death. Deep sorrow and honest grief are part of this experience. Death ends a life, but the relationship lives on with the surviving spouse who feels the emptiness that the deceased leaves behind. How difficult it has been for one of my clients whose husband died recently. She expressed her sorrow:

At dinner time, I still place two dishes on the table and his flowery napkin next to his dish. I eat alone as silence responds to my endless questions. I look around and see volumes of his books. Sometimes I think I see him sitting in his favorite chair, reading; he was an avid reader. The rooms remain empty. I look at his picture on the wall and think, *I wish he had not died so soon.* I turn off the light and silence fills the house. Loneliness and pain creep into my heart.

What brought some comfort and gradually a resolution to her grief was the memory of the good life experiences that the spouses shared with love and affection over the years.

For Christian people, death is not an end. Life is not taken away. Death exists but only for a moment. Our physical body returns back to earth from whence it came and our soul leaves the temporal and enters the eternal. It is a starting point of a new life in the presence of God, in whose presence we will all ultimately be.

THOUGHTS TO CONSIDER:

- Transitions in life are inevitable. Endless physical and emotional changes take place and challenge us to let go of familiar experiences, accept something different, and sometimes expect the unexpected. Married couples, individually and together, go through transitions that cause anxiety.
- Even in the best of relationships, spouses' ways of being and their lifestyles go through adjustments and readjustments that are necessary for growth. Love and respect are being tested; if there is genuine love for each other the couple endures the hardships in anticipation of a better life.
- As spouses try to adjust to every new stage of married life, doubts may enter their minds; these tend to be difficult times, because they mark new beginnings. If spouses value

their relationship they will sense inner energy to pursue and welcome yet another new beginning—even during a critical time.

- In little ways spouses must learn to be mindful of each other's needs and develop a caring attitude for their relationship. Amazing growth and maturity take place as spouses discover a viable balance in their interaction, not in competition with each other but in caring cooperation.

- Married life invites a man and a woman to take the path of reality—marriage means responsibility and accountability. Each spouse has to be alert and sensitive to what it takes to make each stage of the marriage better. At the same time, each spouse must enable the other to find personal fulfillment for their individual lives as well as for their relationship.

CHAPTER 5

Expectations

Marriage is never easy. Two individuals cannot expect to be of one mind and one feeling in every instance. However, when the differences threaten the stability of what you have built together, it is time to pause, take another look at your common values and reconsider your expectations.

Dr. Robin L. Smith

All humans enter the state of married life or a significant relationship with a number of expectations. Some of these are tenderly verbalized with expectations of fulfillment, and others remain unexpressed. In marriage, as certain needs are being fulfilled and adjustments are being made, new needs emerge. Each spouse continuously appears to have additional expectations. Initially, spouses may act sacrificially to meet the other's needs, because the pounding heart, racing blood, and romantic feelings fuel the desire to please. What happens when those feelings diminish and expectations seem to increase? At times, expectations are not met because one spouse does not know what is expected of him or her. Sexual encounters in married life are good examples of situations in which expectations differ. When the wife needs to be held and touched affectionately, instantly the husband, misinterpreting her expectation, expects sexual fulfillment. That is not what the wife had in mind, and it is not a good time for her to satisfy his need.

When husbands and wives do not respect each other's sexual expectations, they ignore a very important part of married life. Perhaps, a woman's most important expression of love—from a man's point of view—is her commitment to a mutually fulfilling sexual relationship. Surveys consistently indicate that sex is one of a man's most important needs—if not *the* most important. When a wife demonstrates resistance, only mild interest, or active disinterest, her husband may feel rejected. The responses, *Not now, dear,* or *I'm very tired,* or *I have a headache,* consciously or subconsciously, are interpreted by the husband as rejection or as, *She doesn't care or love me anymore.* Rejection causes withdrawal, and in many cases it encourages infidelity. A better approach to meeting expectations may be to verbalize each expectation one at a time and with a gentle spirit. Expectations could be effectively met when we choose the right time and the right place to discuss them.

Let's take a serious look at a few expectations, find an appropriate way to clarify them, and see how can they be met realistically.

1. Togetherness: As desirable as it may seem to be together and do things together all the time, in the course of married life there are other tasks requiring individual attention. Your personal interests may oblige you to mingle with people other than your spouse. Each of you may seek a colleague or a friend with whom to pursue an activity that may exclude the other. This is not done intentionally in order to avoid your partner. It simply points out the need to connect with other people to feel fully human and fully alive.

2. Physical and Emotional Closeness: Obviously there is frequent and intense closeness prior to marriage. Once you are married, closeness takes a different form; it becomes a more relaxed and rewarding experience. The intensity of sexual encounters is often reduced, and it is time to develop a dialogue with each other. Things need to be done; chores must be accomplished. Somebody has to go shopping for food and household items; somebody has to cook or do the cleaning and attend to the maintenance of the home. Someone has to balance the checkbook and pay the bills. When these routines are discussed and shared, each partner pitches in to facilitate life and living. There is no reason why these physical tasks cannot be within the realm of closeness.

3. Agreement: Seeing eye-to-eye with each other on everything that comes your way may be difficult. Two different people with different values, different backgrounds, and different sets of habits cannot possibly agree on all of life's unfolding experiences. One person enjoys climbing mountains; the other prefers swimming in the ocean. One is gregarious and loves to socialize; the other is an introvert and prefers solitude. One expresses anger openly; the other represses anger and withdraws. Of course such differences cause confusion or discomfort, but do they have to cause conflict? Do they have to be the cause of a battle? Consider the possibility of accepting the other person as being different from you. Does your spouse have to agree with everything that you say and do? Our minds constantly create mental models of how things should be, how problems should be solved, and how others should behave. Such ideas are almost always different from what is—they can be different from reality. Despite your persistent effort to *change your spouse* to match your images or your perceptions, your spouse will continue to live life in his or her own way. The key to your marital success is learning *adaptation*, that is, accepting and adapting to each other's ways, facilitating each other's growth, maintaining integrity, and moving forward without one trying to control or manipulate the other.

4. Unconditional Love: Most marriages originate with the partners having a sense of adoration for each other. Each spouse being intensely in love cannot do enough to satisfy the other. Later, as life moves on, this type of intensity is converted into focus on the marriage. The best way to help your partner to experience greater love for you is to create in yourself an experience of greater love for him or her. Create a spirit of loving without expecting a return, without a bookkeeping approach, *I have done this for you, so you now owe me something.* Love does not work effectively when you expect repayment. You love your spouse because he or she is there for you, not because your spouse needs, merits, or deserves your love. Take a minute and look deeply into your heart to discover your level of love and commitment to the well-being of your partner. True love does not consist in gazing at each other, but in looking outward together in the same direction.

5. All Needs Met: It is humanly impossible to fulfill all the needs of your spouse. No man or woman could possibly meet the other's needs 100 percent. Start with an effort to achieve 10 percent fulfillment of your spouse's needs, and let your spouse develop his or her individual skills of self-fulfillment. Ask for what you want, enjoy what your spouse gives you, and work on differences. Both of you need to live in a larger social world—your community, your church, your temple, your friends, personal interests—to draw on resources outside the marriage as well as inside for life and love. When you try to make your spouse your total source of fulfillment, he or she will feel drained, and sooner or later life will be troublesome; either one or both of you will be running for your lives!

6. My Love Will Change My Spouse: People usually mature, but seldom do they change. It would be ideal if your love *could* change all the undesirable qualities that you see in your spouse. Marriage is a planted garden. Observe its growth and facilitate it by removing the thistles and weeds. If you want fruits, then you must nurture, prune, and cultivate your garden. Your personal life and the relationship require similar attention. If love means acceptance and acceptance implies tolerance, learn not to complain about your mate's character defects. The hardest things to change or eliminate are the bad habits. Try using *prefer* requests. They are more effective. For example:

I prefer that we rise earlier in the morning and share a few minutes together before we go to work.

I prefer that on Saturday morning we have breakfast together, instead of separately. This quiet meal together would make me feel connected with you for the rest of the busy day.

I prefer that once a week we go food shopping together. Then we could buy items that we both need.

I prefer to be on time when we visit friends; I know it's not a big issue, but being on time makes me feel more comfortable. Would you mind leaving a few minutes earlier next time?

I prefer that we have a candlelight dinner at home every other Friday. It would be a good time for us to catch up with whatever is going on in our lives and a time to make plans for the weekend.

The above *prefer* requests may prove beneficial in maintaining a stronger relationship in your marriage. Each *prefer* request needs to be reality based and said with tender love.

7. Marriage Cures All Ills: It does not. You have a temper, and once you get married you think you will be able to control it; often you cannot. Nobody can deal with a spouse that throws temper tantrums. If you are a jealous person, displays of bad temper may be an indication of insecurity and a desire to be in charge of your spouse's feelings. Replace your jealous feelings with trust. That is, trust yourself to be your best and trust your spouse will be his or her best, too. In married life, jealousy can slowly destroy a relationship. Replace jealousy with love. You are stubborn and tend to be opinionated; once you believe in something, no one can change your mind. You may be saying to yourself, *I'm entitled to my opinions.* Sure you are, but keep them to yourself. If you impose your opinions or feelings of distrust on your spouse, how do you expect your spouse to feel toward you? Of course there will be disagreements, flare-ups, and even conflicts. Do they have to put down or destroy the other? Do you have to be in control of your mate with your attitude? What about having a serious discussion and arriving together at a realistic solution? You will always have issues that will need resolution, and sometimes you may agree to disagree.

When you realize that you have hurt your spouse's feelings, learn to apologize. Admitting that you did something wrong does not make you weak or inferior. It makes you an honest person. Learn also to forgive yourself for the possible hurt that you may have caused. Get rid of your guilt, for negative feelings prevent growth. If each partner allows the other to verbalize what hurts, then each can contribute toward solutions that heal wounds. Solutions must be balanced so that neither feels defeated. If you feel hurt, learn to forgive. Forgiveness can soften the heart and drain the bitterness.

8. Future Plans: Like most people you have entered married life with a personal agenda. You verbalized certain wishes to your spouse, and as your needs were met you gradually came up with more wants and expectations. This happened because initially many of your needs were fulfilled: love, companionship, friendship, cooperation, and sexuality. However, as time moved on and you reached the middle years, more needs surfaced, and you want to see them satisfactorily met:

PERHAPS:

You want a nicer and more comfortable home.

You would even like to have a vacation house.

You would like to reconnect with your relatives.

You want to travel and see other parts of the world.

You want to develop new friends with whom you would enjoy sharing time.

You may be bored and need a different job or a different hobby.

You may want to complete your education.

You may need to get involved in physical activity.

You may need time out to be with old friends.

As you get older, your expectations tend to change, and what appeared to be so important a year ago loses its significance a year later. Marriage becomes stronger as we openly discuss our changing needs and reach a solution satisfactory to both.

THOUGHTS TO CONSIDER:

- Your mate is your mate, the one whom you chose to marry. If you want him or her to be different from what he or she is, then you are in trouble. Can you tell an apple to become an orange because you prefer oranges and orange juice? If you do not like apples, then pluck your fruit from an orange tree. Why not enjoy the apple? It is all a matter of attitude.

- Although you cannot control all the events of your married life, you can control your attitude toward your relationship. Once you accept yourself, it is easier to accept your partner. The next step is to accept responsibility for your behavior. Finally, see what contributions you are making toward your life together and how you are meeting your common expectations.

- Unquestionably, you would like to be happy. A good relationship is never accidental. It is a vigilant process of applying constructive skills. A determination must be made with regard to time spent together and the way it is appropriated. Instead of spending leftover time with each other, you should plan how to have key time together. It is the quality of time that counts, not the quantity.

- Planning and time-management strategies are tools to utilize carefully. Planning is a two-step process. First, identify your mutual expectations. Second, establish your priorities. What is it that needs immediate attention? When both of you have established your priorities, you can begin to organize your time so that what you are choosing to do is compatible with priorities you have set.

- Goals and priorities do change at different times. It is important to take time to support each priority as it surfaces. If one partner is dissatisfied with the way things are going in the marriage, then, before any new priorities are pursued, it is imperative that your partner's dissatisfaction be resolved. Acknowledge the dissatisfaction and see if you can sensitively encourage a discussion about it; should your partner be reluctant to talk, do not press the issue. Another way to handle the matter is to say, *I'm sorry you're sad; have I hurt your feelings?* Or, *I'll be in the next room. When you feel like talking, please join me.*

- It is important for every couple to spend time together, a minimum of twenty minutes each day, practicing a daily dialogue. This type of interaction contributes toward a more mature and rewarding relationship. What oxygen is to the body, dialogue is to the soul. Allow a period of time during your daily life to share feelings, thoughts, ambitions, and plans with your mate. In spending time together you discover the better qualities that you both have.

CHAPTER 6

Assumptions and Reality

When two imperfect and incompatible people, a man and a woman, make a commitment to stay together through a constant effort of love, they have a strong marriage.

José de Vinck

Married life becomes troublesome when each spouse assumes that the other knows what to say or what is expected. Reality indicates that communications get blurred when dialogue becomes an argument. *Communicate* literally means *to become one with,* to make a heart-to-heart connection that gives evidence of who you are and who the other is. There is always a fear that you may be misunderstood or even criticized by the other. In view of your emotional sensitivity as a spouse, take full responsibility for your own thoughts, feelings, actions, and reactions. Do not assume that your spouse is always aware or knows what you are thinking or how you are feeling or what it is that you want. No human being has the ability to read minds. Your spouse is not a difficult person because he or she fails to fulfill your wishes. Instead of assuming that your spouse should know what you want, you may have a better relationship if, in a friendly and loving way, you express your wishes. The following example illustrates this point.

Andy and Debby had been married for eleven years and, as they both approached their mid-thirties, they began to have unrealistic expectations. They had similar backgrounds—both had experienced serious deprivation in their early lives, which brought them closer during their three-year courtship. They expected their marriage would make up for their earlier deprivation. It is impossible for one human being to fulfill all verbalized or unverbalized expectations of another.

Each came to marital therapy angry because the marriage did not turn out to be what they had expected—a happy one.

"He knew me, so he should *know* what I want," Debby said.

"I've tried to make our marriage a good one, but whatever I do, I don't seem able to please her. I guess I've failed," Andy said in utter frustration.

"There are so many things that you don't care to do."

"What things?" Andy interrupted, his voice raised.

"Well, you never come home and suggest that we go out and have fun," she complained.

"Did you ever tell him what kind of fun you would like?" I inquired.

"He should know what I want."

"How should I know? I don't read minds," Andy interrupted, irritated.

"We have been married for eleven years, and we knew each other three years before that; isn't that enough time to know what I want?" Debby blurted out.

This question was met with prolonged silence. Andy, shaking his head, kept looking through the window. Then Debby said, "If he really loved me, he would be sensitive and understand my needs."

Debby viewed her desire to go out and have fun as one of her needs. It was obviously a strong *wish*, but hardly a need. She had *decided* that he did not love her because he had not been able to read her mind. He had decided that she was so irrational that there was nothing he could do that would satisfy her. Andy and Debbie had made *decisions* that made their communication a series of angry attacks on each other. As a result, their relationship suffered.

Statements such as, *If he loves me he should know what makes me happy,* or *If she loves me, she should not make demands on me,* become major obstacles to good communication. It is difficult for many people to accept the fact that their needs are not instantly communicated. What may seem obvious to one has to be expressed accurately if the wish is to be understood and met by the other spouse.

The statement, *If we truly love one another, we will always know what the other wants,* is erroneous logic. No one can read another's mind and know the other's thoughts, feelings, wishes, and needs. Love is not omniscient. Love implies a desire to be beneficially present in the life of another. It does seek to understand and to contribute to the happiness of a significant other. The focus is on working toward the attainment of cooperation and harmony. Couples who aspire toward realistic, expressed goals find joy in their relationship.

The secret is to avoid doing destructive things. Most people stumble at times during their married life; they make mistakes. Yet mistakes become lasting lessons, and making the same mistakes proves to be unwise. As we began to work together, Andy and Debby realized it was safe to talk more openly. When I asked each of them to express openly what he or she resented about the other, Andy turned to his wife and said, "I wish you wouldn't fall all over my friends and giggle all the time when we go out!"

"What are you talking about?" Debby's face turned red. "You must be jealous," she said.

"Maybe I am."

"Well, grow up. I only wanted your friends to accept me. And I tried to be pleasant."

"My friends like you. You don't have to fall all over them."

This pattern occurred early in their marriage. Andy wanted his wife to be sociable and accepted by his friends. Debby was merely trying to please him. Her actions, however, did not meet his expectations. Both had failed to convey accurately what they expected from each other.

Definite progress was made when Andy spoke openly about his jealousy and began to understand his insecurity as a man and a husband. Jealously is an insidious enemy to married life. It has caused extramarital affairs, fights, and divorces. I plan to elaborate on the topic of jealousy in another chapter.

Debby, on the other hand, came to realize that her behavior toward Andy's friends was rather flirtatious and could invite trouble. Gradually, her expectation surfaced. "I want Andy to be more affectionate toward me, and pay attention to me even when we're with his friends."

Each learned to speak openly, conveying clear messages about their individual needs and desires, and Debby stopped being flirtatious. Andy then showed greater regard for Debby's feelings.

This is just one example, but it demonstrates how vitally important healthy communication can be for both partners, enabling them to understand what they are doing to themselves and to each other. Only then can they move from discord to harmony. How most couples usually relate in different aspects of their marriage is a major issue. As singles, each handled personal affairs according to individual preferences with no accountability to anyone. As a married couple, each spouse has to be accountable to the other. Pertinent to the marriage, neither can make decisions arbitrarily. *How* do they reach each other? *How* do they make major decisions? *How* do they manage money, food preparation, social activities and entertainment, hobbies, religious activities, and sexual life? All these facets need to be resolved with mutual concern and respect and open communication.

How we do things and interact with each other is called the *process* of marital life. This is a basic thought to keep in mind. Honest assessment of marital interaction is of prime importance. Each problem that emerges requires solution, but the chief focus remains on *how* to enrich the marriage through each interaction. Within the context of a marriage in which each spouse values the other and the relationship, constructive methods for dealing with disagreements ought to be considered.

If warfare, either overt or covert, occurs each time a decision needs to be made, husband and wife pull away from each other, each thinking that he or she knows the right solution. Negative feelings develop and the warfare results in torment and a sense of entrapment. Self-esteem is threatened. Feelings of mutual respect and consideration, of loving and being loved, suffer slow death. Each spouse begins to feel isolated, victimized, betrayed, angry, and depressed. Each is alone, struggling with the demons of avoidance and alienation. Examining alternatives and making cooperative decisions are major parts of a sensitive *process*. For many couples, the process becomes a power struggle that hinders growth. Who is going to win? Who will have the last word? Who will prevail? Who is right and who is wrong? My favorite line to couples that engage in power struggles is, *Do you want to prove that you are right or do you want to stay married?* Reality tells us that in married life no spouse can claim superiority over the other or be the only winner. Both either win or lose together. A good thing to keep in mind is to avoid antagonisms.

Marriages consist of imperfect people living in an imperfect world. Instead of feeling frustration, disappointment, and pain, a positive path to follow would be to use each mistake as a stepping-stone to a higher marital plain. Stop and think; success comes and goes, but a mistake is a lesson that stays. You must have heard the axiom, *Every success is built on a pyramid of failures.* Whether or not a couple grows and matures beyond the challenges of married life depends upon their willingness to work hard at their marriage.

Some couples who start out with passionate love become confused, angry, or helpless when passion subsides. If they choose to examine their feelings, perhaps with professional help, love may become a reality once more. Other partners who are chronically in conflict and are unwilling to seek help and face themselves endure much pain. There is not much hope for such couples. Eventually, they have to make a decision about which direction to take—toward marital death or toward renewed marital life.

Sometimes partners reach a point that leads to a destructive impasse: *I'm really stuck. I have children to think of. I can't work. I guess this is my fate. It's terrible. It's awful. I should have listened to my parents; they didn't want me to marry this woman. If my situation doesn't improve, I'll have a nervous breakdown. I don't see any way out.*

Many distraught partners are painfully aware that their relationship has become anemic, but they are not aware that their flawed interaction is causing its demise. It is through the *how* that spouses either maintain a loving relationship or destroy it. If each marriage is to survive happily, each spouse must feel that the other is making a concerted effort to improve the relationship. There is no substitute for honest, nondefensive confrontation and communication.

The key is to use mature and serious dialogue. During courtship, there usually is no problem talking; dialogue is eloquent and endless, interesting, but not necessarily pertinent to major issues. Attraction, hormones, and romantic encounters overshadow future concerns and responsibilities. In marriage, dialogue dwindles when important matters—maintaining a loving relationship, earning a living, making home life pleasant, meeting financial obligations—are no longer discussed. When husbands and wives are silent and neither knows what the other is thinking, often a personal dialogue is going on internally. Ongoing silence can be damaging, for it is only through open dialogue that one gets to know the other and understands what the relationship needs.

Another common problem occurs when one decides, *I deserve better*, not really having a clear picture of what he or she wants. This does not mean that this partner believes he or she is a perfect person. Rather, it usually means that a decision has been made that a better life is deserved, at least much better than what exists.

For example, some husbands begin to feel that their wives should be more attractive, more articulate, better homemakers, better mothers. Some wives think that their husbands should be more caring, more intelligent, more successful, and better lovers. This is related to an early belief, actually a fantasy, that a marriage will meet all expectations and, obviously, that each partner will have this *better* life. They look at each other, feeling deprived of what they deserve. Then comes the ambivalence about the marriage itself. Such turmoil requires candor, confrontation, and enlightenment. A marriage therapist can help a couple reach a decision by observing the marriage from both points of view. An awakening occurs when each realizes how little real attention has been given to the partner, how engrossed he or she has been in *their own world*, and how rigid each has

47

been in defending his or her own position. Such situations often lead to serious disagreements that precipitate other dissatisfactions that, in turn, cause more frustration. When the relationship is going smoothly, it is easy to forget that the loved one has family, friends, career responsibilities, and social obligations. All these are remembered when decision making occurs. *Who executes plans? How? When? What?*

Marriage consists of three components—each important, each having a flow of its own, and each making the other possible. They are:

1. My partner
2. The relationship
3. Myself

When these components are in harmony the marriage functions smoothly. Love, good feelings, joy, and progress can flourish only when all three components of married life have room to grow and no one part dominates or absorbs the other. When each partner has a feeling of self-worth and each expresses this feeling to the other in a nondemanding manner, a worthwhile relationship will develop.

Marriage requires that spouses take the path of the inner truth—and that means taking responsibility for *everything* pertinent to the relationship. *What pleases our partner and what pleases us—for the good part inside us and for the bad part?* Through a friendly dialogue with our partner, we discover those good and bad parts are different from each other, and we should respect them.

In a harmonious marriage, actions communicate in a thousand different ways that the marital relationship really matters. The husband who calls home to say he will be a half hour late is saying, *I'm thinking of you even though I had a hectic day today.* When in-laws, a friend, or a neighbor phones three minutes before dinner, the wife who says, *I'll call you back later,* instead of delaying dinner by talking on the phone, sends a clear message about her priorities to both the caller and to her husband.

Spouses who arrange their weekly schedule to include a date with each other without the children have said a lot about their relationship. In public, some husbands are reluctant to show affection by holding hands or putting an arm around their wives. Why? It is not unmanly when, in the presence of others, a husband makes an affirmative action that most wives appreciate. This physical gesture says, *This is the woman that I love,* or *I am the man she loves.*

When the wife says, *I'm sorry I was so insensitive last night when you told me that your boss praised you. You were so happy! I did not even congratulate you to share your joy. Our marriage is precious to me even though at times I may not tell you. I apologize.* Even if the wife's reaction is delayed, it shows love and sensitivity to her husband's life.

Hiding our real feelings because they might be negative perpetuates the illusion of tranquillity. Spouses who are willing to listen to each other, sharing enthusiasm or frustration, or listening to the story of the day's unhappy events without giving advice or criticism are making a strong affirmation: *Our relationship is very important.* The rationale that the other will not or cannot understand the truth may merely be a handy excuse for avoiding meaningful communication. Couples who learn to relate feelings, ideas, ambitions, and plans to each other in a positive manner truly experience surprising results.

THOUGHTS TO CONSIDER:

- If you notice that your behavior causes trouble or emotional pain, you should make an effort to change it. Consider how much your relationship suffers because of these patterns and remember that you are the only one who *can* change destructive, counterproductive behavior to constructive behavior.
- Marital interaction often becomes blurred. Husbands and wives cannot clearly see what long-term damage may result from angry discourse. Either they are angry because something undesirable has happened between

them or they are facing a serious obstacle. At such times it is wise to reexamine the situation and not make any decisions until after a period of rest, reflection, and reassessment.

- Personal or marital growth is attainable as you consider your human condition, strengths, and weaknesses. It is of benefit to see yourselves as human beings and to see your partner as a human being as well. Perfection in personal behavior is an ideal not to be attained on earth, but it can be improved if you really want to be happy.

- Spouses are responsible for the growth of their marriage. Everyone is endowed with a body, mind, and soul. If you use these endowments constructively, they are sources of great help. Saying to your spouse, *I love you*, is very important. It is even of great importance to your marriage to make an effort to become consistently loving mates.

- Perfection in marriage is an ideal, and cannot be attained on earth, regardless of how hard you try. Yet, a life of harmony and love between spouses is attainable and meaningful. At your best, give your mate the opportunity to explore who he or she is and enable your marriage to become all that God intends.

CHAPTER 7

Finding Harmony

Harmony lies in the ability to see human imperfection as one of the realities of life, and to act willingly, thoughtfully, and cooperatively in ways that promote compassion, love, respect, and good will among partners.

Edward E. Ford

It took me three full hours to write this particular chapter. When I tried to save it, something went terribly wrong. The whole chapter totally disappeared. Maybe I pressed the wrong key of the computer and erased it, or the topic *Marital Harmony* may be so complex that it should be left unexplored. After a long pause and serious thought, I felt the urge to explore this topic anyway, regardless of how difficult it is to be in harmony with ourselves and with others.

Like love or peace, harmony is a desirable state in any relationship, especially in the institution of marriage. It is a challenge for those who are willing to work for it. Most married people might raise the question, *Is there such a thing as marital harmony?* It is a good question that may be combined with many more questions: *Why is it that so many spouses who claim to love one another cause emotional hurricanes and storms? Why do we verbally attack people that we love? Why are we so irritable? Why do we overreact to a slight provocation to the point of rage? Could it be that certain experiences keep poking into the present?* All these questions that surface in our minds create a challenge for us. We need viable answers.

51

Those of us who plan to continue our married life harmoniously need to understand fully the realities of marriage.

Starting with thoughts and reflections on the masculine-feminine phenomenon and on how a man and a woman interact with each other, what do we notice? Men and women become committed to a relationship. What determines their everyday behavior? To put it more specifically: *What are couples looking for in married life? What efforts do they need to employ to get what is really desired from the marriage and from the person they have married?* To get the things that you want out of your marriage, the first step is for you to decide what you want and be willing to work for it.

The activities of animals are determined in part by inborn patterns of behavior and by external stimuli. In the spring, for example, certain stimuli cause some species of birds to build nests according to a specific design. As soon as the eggs hatch and the parents see the open beaks of the fledglings, the behavioral pattern of feeding is activated.

Humans are different. Although we, too, carry within us inherent ways of behaving, we are different in that we are culturally conditioned to behave in ways wherein the reward for our behavior is our objective. The patterns of behavior among humans are more complicated and less precise than are those of animals. In addition, human patterns of behavior seem to be more numerous, and all of them are not utilized in the course of married life; many remain dormant. Finally, the human being is capable of observing these patterns of behavior, then responding and reflecting on them. Human beings become aware of patterns and make efforts to improve upon them or even change them.

If I could emerge out of these pages and look at your relationship and how you interact with each other with complete impartiality and fairness, I might see something like the following: living together are two people of different sex, perhaps of different culture, different religious background, and different upbringing. You have different images, fantasies, expectations, and myths. You differ in strength and vitality, and possibly have different goals. Because each one loved the other, you exchanged promises to be together for life, to care, to share, and to enjoy aspects of common interest. Neither judges the other's experience; neither controls the other; both need to develop your individual potential. Your marriage oath was declared either at the altar or at the office of a justice of the peace. Because of your love and attraction to each other, you made a decision to share a life together.

The Creator instilled these wonderful feelings in each of us for purposes of procreation and for the pursuit of love and happiness. We may wonder what will happen to our relationship when we need to face the realities and difficulties of married life. Will we ignore them and try to avoid or escape our responsibilities? Will we expect our spouse to do what we need to do ourselves? Or will we label the spouse we claim to love as *the difficult one?*

Most people know that living with another person creates tension, discomfort, disagreement, and conflict. Part of being human implies that we cannot always have things our way. However, married partners have promised to live together for their whole lives in order to promote the greatest physical, spiritual, and psychological intimacy possible.

Most people made this promise at a time when their physical and emotional attractions were at their peak and sexual desire was seeking to be satisfied. At that time, neither of the partners knew what sort of person the other was about to evolve and develop into in later years. The charming adaptable young girl, the unique and gorgeous female suddenly might become— who would guess it—a power freak? She might evolve into a controlling, insecure, manipulating, nagging wife. The romantic young man, the charming and handsome lover who had such lofty plans and who made promises of happiness for the future might turn into an spineless weakling, a selfish, demanding, egocentric, chauvinistic husband.

What happened to love and loving? Time and different needs that surfaced day by day impose a new type of stress that you do not experience during the romantic premarital days. Once you are married, possibly for several years, you can no longer return to your own bachelor home to rest and regain strength after a hot date. The marital Garden of Eden that you once dreamed about is nonexistent. Now you have your own garden that needs constant care if you hope to have flowers and fruit. After a pleasant evening, you return together to your own home only to be reminded of domestic duties and responsibilities that are part of your life together. Couples need to pamper one another. In a good relationship, couples find time for every task and for every need.

We cannot overlook the fact that we are human and, as such, we are imperfect. Consequently, the best of us will still have an imperfect marriage, and that is normal. Remember, as mature as we claim to be, we try in our own way, with more or less success, to wrestle with the fundamental, insoluble problems and contradictions of life, such as the longing to be cared for, the enjoyment of childish dependency on one hand and independent existence on the other. We want to be free from parents and parental control, and at the same time, we wish to remain children forever. We want to socialize with other couples, but we are unsure of their impression of us, and that makes us apprehensive, and our impression of them causes emotional detachment. We feel anxious over pain, illness, and aging. The fear of death and the aspiration for longer life become our preoccupations.

Truly, in spite of what your experiences have been until now, you have a chance to remodel your marriage and make it work. How? Even if you have tried and have failed to make it work before, now turn your failure into a lesson. Do not listen to the many voices of friends or relatives. Listen to the voice of God that comes to us through the mouth of St. Paul the Apostle. In his Epistle to the Romans, he says, "*Do not be conformed to this world, but be transformed by the renewing of your minds, so that you may discern what is the will of God—what is good and acceptable and perfect*" (Rom 12:2). Choose not external opinions or lifestyles. Choose not the angry or the frustrated part of yourself, but the healthy part that is capable of loving and forgiving. Forgiveness may help your spouse, but its primary purpose is to free you. If you are hurt and feel angry, do not let anger control you; learn to forgive.

Lewis Smedes described it well when he said, "*Nobody seems to be born with much talent of forgiving. We all need to learn from scratch, and the learning to forgive almost always runs against the grain. Most of us do not want to let go of hurts or wrongs done to us. We want revenge or at least to get even. Honestly, what does such an attitude accomplish?"*

Dwelling on what hurts you is a type of self-inflicted wound, self-flagellation, in which your attention and energy are focused on the thoughts, *Why did this happen to me? It should not have happened. It was unfair.* As justified as these statements may be, in what way do they help you to regain peace in your life?

Ideally, two mentally stable individuals make a strong marriage. However, reality indicates it rarely happens that two completely healthy people get together. It is a common occurrence to find that each has neurotic needs, peculiarities, and distortions. Marriage does not have to do with curing or changing the other significantly; this is not possible, but marriage *can* be a clinic where healing is available. The curing is in the hands of God.

You may recall that through the decision to get married you have taken on the task of mutual confrontation with life's experiences until death. Your marriage can work, but the human shortcomings have to be reconsidered and refined. Character differences between partners have to be balanced to complement each other, and personal peculiarities have to be resolved, accepted, and integrated into positive interaction with your spouse. The keyword is *flexibility*, a virtue in a viable marriage. You need to accept yourself and accept your spouse. In spite of your strong convictions, you must allow your spouse to have his or her own views and not expect such views to be totally in agreement with yours. You may agree to disagree when you perceive things differently.

The inability to see the truth about one's self causes an ongoing turbulent life that surfaces in many significant relationships. Either you accept who you really are and accept your spouse and be at peace, or you suffer slow emotional deterioration. Gerald May, MD, emphasizes the point: *"Always there is a desire to accept some things and reject others. Who is making this choice and with what wisdom? Does one accept what feels good and reject what does not? Total, complete acceptance is a very real possibility."*

In marriage, we learn to find meaning by extending grace and acceptance to a spouse who has seemingly wronged us. If we learn to accept and forgive our imperfect spouse, we become well equipped to practice both acceptance and forgiveness outside of our marriage. These acts may seem unnatural—it takes awareness and discipline in practicing them.

Mature love is a state in which the satisfaction and security of another person become as important as your own. It bespeaks a relationship of mutual trust and respect, and it allows for the expression of the maximum potentialities of each person for giving and receiving. In the state of love there is respect, trust, concern, and affection for the other person—not simply mutual sexual interaction or a business transaction. One does not only give and the other does not only take, but both partners give and receive. This is not an idealized formula of a harmonious marriage. It is the reality of a good marriage.

The accomplishments of our times are the results of dreams and ideas that scientists pursued. After trials and errors, the dreams became realities. If harmony in your marriage seems a dream, should you not make an effort to make it a reality? If you do not, who will? If not now, when do you think you can make an effort to bring harmony into your life?

Marriage is an opportunity to share life with another human being. This is truly one of life's greatest challenges. However, high expectations can easily damage and stifle our efforts to have a good marriage. A spouse may say, *I expect you to make me happy*. Unquestionably, such a demand causes pressure or even guilt for the other spouse. Instead of expecting the other to make you happy—an impossible task—try to find happiness within yourself, and feel good in your partner's presence.

Think of an expectation, a demand that you are making. When your spouse fails to fulfill your demand—because of timing or personal agenda or disposition—your emotion-backed, unmet demand may automatically trigger anger, irritation, fear, resentment, boredom, or even grief. Simply stated, external reality triggers an internal reservoir of feelings. If you choose to blame your spouse for lack of sensitivity to your needs, the wall between the two of you becomes higher.

When you begin to like yourself and become lovable, your partner will find it a pleasure to be in your company. Then you are giving your partner a healthy, happy person to cherish and love. You can get love from your spouse by extending yourself, even if it means acting contrary to the way you feel. Instead of being a taker, you become a giver. It is a sign of maturity when you are able to give love to others. In order to do this, you must have your physical, emotional, and spiritual needs met. As Christians, we have a great opportunity to have our needs met. Jesus meets all our needs. He says, "*Strive first for the kingdom of God and his righteousness, and all these things*"—*food, clothing, shelter and emotional support*—"*will be given to you...* " (Matt 6:33). Our Lord meets our emotional needs. His voice comes to us through the writings of St. Paul. "*Who shall separate us from the love of God?*" (Rom 8:35).

God provides us with all the love, attention, and acceptance we need. We are loved with his everlasting love, so we can respond to others, primarily to our spouses, out of that love. This is both our choice and our most rewarding challenge.

Stop for a moment. Take a profound look into your heart to discover your level of commitment to the person you have married. Be totally realistic. Love does not work when you expect to get something. You love your spouse because he or she is there, not because he or she needs, merits, or deserves your love. When you love someone, you are tuned into your beloved's relationship to his or her own life and not narrowly concerned with his or her relationship to your life.

From time to time, your partner's well-being may have needs on which you do not want to spend money, energy, or time. If it really affects your partner's happiness, make a decision. What are your limits? Doing a little something for the other or buying a small gift may not guarantee happiness, but it surely facilitates the spirit of wellness in your marriage. Avoid the bookkeeping approach: *I have done this for you, so you now owe me something.* In the course of a week, two people living together may make many contributions to each other's mutual well-being. These can take the form of energy put into helping one another by cooking, serving, dishwashing, shopping, house-cleaning, doing yard work, maintaining the car, assisting when sickness occurs, playing host to a friend, doing thoughtful deeds, suggesting a good book to read, going to a movie or concert, and cooperating in sexual enjoyment.

Enjoying what is available in your present day is most important. Avoid the *I-need-more* mentality. Excess has rarely made anyone happy. Our culture truly victimizes people with the *more* madness. As a couple, you don't need more to be happy. Just enjoy each other with the spirit of *enoughness*. Be grateful for what you have today. What you have this very moment suffices for this particular day. It is time to open your heart to harmony and happiness by not creating *negative notions* of what you do not have. Like a conductor of a concert who coordinates a number of instruments to produce a melody, try to combine all the elements of your life together to pursue a life of harmony.

A secure way to contribute to each other's well-being must include handling your own *personal priorities* and creating emotional space for your partner to dissipate frustration, anger, fear, jealousy, irritation, resentment, depression, and other divisive emotional states, even when they are directed toward you. Contributing to each other's joy could also include helping your partner to do what he or she wants to do, compassionately understanding tension areas, and sharing your innermost feelings sensitively.

The joy of living together can only reach its highest fruition when our psyche has insight into physical, mental, and spiritual wellness and develops an attitude of goodwill for the relationship. A negative attitude and a habit of pointing out the deficiencies of your partner push your relationship downhill. It would be more effective to examine your own deficiencies and bring yourself into awareness that, as a human, you are imperfect. Start by being gentle and compassionate with yourself. Relinquish unrealistic demands on yourself or on your spouse. Your spouse is who he or she is—different from you. If you are able to accept yourself as you are, then you can accept the other as he or she is. How really unfair it is to try to change your spouse! Change him or her into what? Make him or her more like you? Is that possible?

Accept without resistance what you cannot change. Intelligently focus your energy on making whatever changes are possible without setting up new problems in your life. If this marriage is not making you happy, you need to delve profoundly into yourself to discover the cause of your unhappiness. Unhappy adults make unhappy marriages. Stop accusing or blaming your spouse for your unhappiness and begin to restore your self-image. In leaving this marriage and starting another one, you have no guarantee that you will not bring your unhappy self into another relationship. Chances are that another marriage will be just as unhappy because, basically, you are an unhappy person.

What makes us unhappy? Some people are genetically unhappy. Nothing pleases them. Their unhappiness is rooted in their childhood; some significant adult or parental figure did not love them sufficiently. It could also be that such unhappy creatures were overloved as children and now, in their adult lives, they cannot find that type of love again. If we exclude physical deficiencies and unbalanced hormones, perhaps we can pinpoint the issue of unhappiness.

When you let go of the notion or demand that your spouse is obligated to make you happy or make your marriage perfect, then you will begin to appreciate the relationship for the richness that it does give you. The greatest richness is that you can absolutely count on your marriage to give you lots of opportunities for growth and maturation. It is up to you to use these opportunities. Your marriage is like a garden; it has all the potential to produce fruits if you are willing to cultivate it.

THOUGHTS TO CONSIDER:

- Personal growth implies that you make a conscious decision to face the realities of your own life, to come to terms with who you really are and what you want out of your life.
- In your marriage, the realization that each person has to maintain a healthy outlook toward the relationship will lead you through the transitions of married life.
- The security and well-being of your spouse has to be as significant as your own security and well-being. At moments of dissatisfaction when you think of divorce, even as a

fleeting thought, could you stop and ask yourself, *Is there a problem-free marriage?* Most marriage and family therapists will say there is no problem-free marriage.

- Two people who decide to live together under the same roof and share common and personal goals, at one time or another will have a disagreement that can result in a conflict. Many people experience marriage as entrapment, a never-ending series of obligations that cause husbands and wives to feel unappreciated. How can you show appreciation for your spouse to avoid this feeling?

- A positive attitude promotes good communications and makes a relationship a pleasant journey toward happiness and rewarding life goals. Negativity, labeling, putdowns, criticism, complaints, and ignoring a mate's needs can gradually destroy a marriage.

- Unless emotionally traumatized or mentally impaired, husbands and wives have the personal power, God's inner gift, to reconstruct their marriage and transform it into the kind of loving relationship that they want to have with each other. While a marriage therapist can help, it takes desire and effort on the part of the couple to work for the marriage. It takes patience, persistence, and prayer for God's guidance.

CHAPTER 8

Do People Change?

> In spite of the changes and variations it suffers,
> nature—in all its glory and perfection—remains con-
> sistent in its basic character. The human character
> reaches a point of "maturity" that it no longer changes.
> All we hope is that humans mature in their minds.
>
> Allen Wheelis

When we take a look at nature, we see its patterns and rhythms;
we see the sun rising and setting; and we observe orchards blos-
soming in springtime and bearing fruit in summer. In autumn,
we see leaves falling to the ground, slowly disintegrating into the
earth, enriching the soil that energizes the trees. Even the cold
winter weather is part of nature's pattern. Nature follows its own
course, ever revealing its amazing majesty, maintaining the consistency of its character. It is inspiring to observe the seasons in
nature as they unfold, gradually and graciously.

Like seasons, humans, during their different phases of life,
go through emotional, physical, intellectual, and spiritual
changes. As part of growth and fulfillment, humans follow cycles
and patterns as paths to maturity. Human beings are endowed
with their own intelligence, idiosyncrasies, growth time, and wisdom. Who can accurately describe the human character? Apart
from the transitions and changes that each person makes, a
sharper look may uncover a consistency of individual character,
inner energy, strength, and vitality, all of which enhance a per-

sonality. During the process of developmental changes, we often face difficulties and opposing forces that may stifle our growth.

Growth means change. Many people are afraid to change because they do not want to appear fickle; they are afraid someone is going to control their lives. Some people are overly concerned about their reputations, about what others think and say about them. Still others believe that changing is admitting the failure of their current lifestyles.

The challenge to change lies in the fact that, not only men and women are different from each other, but that these differences bring conflict as well as comfort. Each gender experiences the differences in a different way, and as spouses bring these differences into the marriage, each feels that the other is the difficult one. The wonder is not that so many do not get along but that so many do. Learning to get along with each other can be a great source of personal growth and happiness.

Allen and Robin, both approaching forty, are still together although their four years of marriage resembled life in a war zone. They had major disagreements, nasty quarrels, and verbal fights; they did not speak to each other for days; they fought *over the silliest things*, they claim. Neither believed in divorce. Both came from Christian backgrounds and attended church regularly, but they did not appear to apply the principles of the Christian faith to their married life. When they sought marital therapy, I asked them what they wanted to see happen in their marriage. Allen volunteered to be the spokesperson.

"Doc, we need major changes in our marriage."

"Major changes?" I asked.

"Yes, sir. I expect my wife to respect me. That's what I need—respect."

"Do you respect her?" I asked with a smile.

"Of course I do," he replied emphatically.

"No Doctor, he does not respect me," Robin interrupted. "He does not like me to have normal contact with my family. When my father phones our home or offers to help us, my husband gets angry."

"Doc, I don't mind her contacting her family, but I object to her discussing our personal issues with her father." Allen's voice was loud and angry.

"Be honest, Allen. Any time I get a phone call you want to know in detail what was said. You analyze everything I do and say, and I'm tired of it." Robin's eyes were brimming with tears.

Allen was a news analyst for a radio station, and his style tended to be carried over into his marriage. However, when he saw his wife in tears, he gave her a tissue and said, "You know I love you. Is it too much to ask you for respect and some accountability?"

It is necessary for a therapist to confront human nature as a source of unhappiness and try to help those in such a situation to overcome it; unfortunately the clients often present resistance. I had to describe what I perceived was blocking the growth of Allen and Robin as honestly as I could to both spouses, individually and in joint therapy. It took three months of weekly sessions that caused emotional pain and also comfort. Allen's insecurity and controlling nature had to be traced and understood as his own personal baggage that he carried from his family of origin. Eventually, what he expected from his wife he himself had to practice. Robin learned not to be so troubled over Allen's analytical mind and to pursue her contacts outside their marriage with discernment and sensitivity. It was not easy for this couple, nor is it easy for any couple, to combat their individual natures; each person is a mystery, and each has to face the forces within. Allen and Robin gradually discovered meaning and purpose in their life together, as they learned to control their own destructive habits and the behavior that affected their relationship.

Among many Christians, there is evidence that change is a creative and rewarding experience. Believers in Christ sense an inward change, a transformation. God's plan for their lives creates an inward change that gradually moves outward, not just an outward conformity. If you are a believer, you may be aware of the process. Already you have a head start toward change. Truly you have a choice, but who is to say how we should shape and live our lives? Each one of us is a unique being; we have choices, and we can follow our own path and design our lifestyle according to our needs. We have personal experience and knowledge, but what we know should not be applied to others, nor should we expect others to see things our way. We have no right to impose our feelings and beliefs on others, nor should we judge others and tell them how to live their lives. Would you like someone else to tell you how to live?

Each day, most of us experience peak periods, moments of enthusiasm when our energy flows the most strongly. There is a time when our character reaches its peak and reveals its distinctive qualities. This is our prime time, a time to pursue the tasks ahead. When our energies diminish and we feel tired and withdrawn, it is time to rest and replenish our energy.

An overwhelmed mind cannot deal effectively with life and may face difficulties in solving major or minor problems. Generally, problem solving is effective when there is desire to have our life in order. There is a sequence to solving our problems. A good way to start is to solve what appears as an easy problem. First, it needs to be defined. Second, a strategy for a solution needs to be developed. Third, the action needs to be performed. Once we solve an easy problem, we gain momentum to solve a more difficult one, applying a similar sequence.

The human mind is like a monkey that jumps from branch to branch to find something interesting and rewarding. As the mind jumps, thoughts hurry, seeking and exploring new attractions. Thoughts determine the way we feel and behave. At times, the mind controls the thoughts; at other times, the thoughts control the mind. If we are to solve any problem, we need to empty the mind of all negative thoughts and focus on the present, examining what is really going on in our life today. Failures and defeats that haunt us can be discouraging when we face difficulties. Failing once or twice does not make our life a failure; rather it teaches us that in the future we must be more careful in our dealings. What can truly help us is to detach ourselves from chaos and confusion.

In problematic relationships, we need to look beneath the surface of our selves. Perhaps it seems easier to break a potentially good relationship or run away from it rather than look deeply into our selves. Intellectual myopia—nearsightedness—tends to be a bane of modern existence. We succumb to quick or easy solutions. Many people waste their time and energy casting blame, perpetuating conflict, and making enemies instead of looking at the entire picture and trying to solve the problems in a prudent and constructive manner.

Sandra and Joel were newlyweds. Their wealthy parents gave them a spectacular wedding attended by 320 guests. Music, hors-d'oeuvres, dinner, and dancing were lavishly presented. The evening extended into the wee hours of the next morning and cost the parents $120,000. For the honeymoon, the young couple took off to explore Africa and enjoy a safari. Six months later, the glamour of the wedding was fading into a pleasant memory. Sandra's mother sensed sadness in her daughter, but she paid little attention to the mood, thinking, *They are newly-weds who have loved each other since their high-school years. They are probably adjusting to their new life.* Sandra, a pampered twenty-one-year-old woman, began to feel uncomfortable in Joel's presence. After the excitement of the wedding day and the honeymoon, she perceived the reality of married life and that scared her. She began to find fault with her husband. *He works too many hours. He spends more time polishing his new car than he spends with me. I don't think he loves me,* were the recurring thoughts that propelled her back to her parents' home. Her mother wondered what had happened to Sandra's love and why her joy at getting married at twenty-one had ceased. Deep down in her heart she knew her daughter had not been ready for a lifetime commitment, but neither she nor her husband had been able to stop the wedding plans. Since their only daughter was determined to get married, they complied with her wishes.

After living with her parents for five months, Sandra sensed a difference in their attitude toward her; she was no longer treated as before—*whatever Sandra wants Sandra gets.* Her parents looked after their own comfort that now included dining out, visiting friends, and traveling to interesting places. Sandra was often left at home feeling lonely. She thought her parents were angry with her for leaving her husband.

Joel maintained the apartment they had rented together. Once a day, he phoned Sandra to see how she was feeling and to ask if he could do anything for her. He said nothing about her coming back to give their married life another chance. She answered Joel's calls in a friendly manner, but she did not give him much hope. Joel loved her, and was hoping that some day Sandra would consider returning to him.

When you and your mate are no longer together and have not talked to each other for a while, it is important not to act compulsively. Instead, take small steps before you run. For example, you cannot expect all of a sudden to either give or receive an invitation to a candlelit gourmet dinner and music in an elegant restaurant. A more practical approach would be to send a card with a message: *I was thinking about you today. Hope you are well. Things are quiet here.* The receiver of your card may see this as an opportunity to respond to you. If there is no response, a few days later, initiate a phone call: *I sent you a card a week ago, and I'm wondering if it has arrived.* The attitude underlying the response you may get will determine whether your conversation should continue or not. If the response is lukewarm, end the conversation gently by saying, *I guess this is not a good time for you. I'll call you another time.*

Sometimes stepping back and carefully assessing what's going on helps to develop personal strength and compassion. You can rediscover the innate wisdom, awareness, and inner joy available in a loving and tender heart. Then you may have to accept your partner and reevaluate your situation wisely, as you consider whether or not you want to spend your life with or without him or her. You may hear, *Don't tell me what to do! This is my life. Don't try to control me.* You have not caused your partner's outburst of anger; rest assured, your mate is defending his or her character and is insisting on maintaining a habitual way of life. This is a reaction that indicates a lack of maturity. Look beneath the surface and choose what is real to you and beneficial to your relationship. When you look at a fruit tree, presumably you admire its shape and blossoms. In reality, it is mainly the fruit that interests you, and the fruit needs to ripen.

Most people who seek therapy are looking for a change in their lives. Sometimes, they want to change the other person, sometimes they want to change themselves. When some people who have self-knowledge feel unhappy with their present life, they want to change how they think, feel, and behave. Their relationship has suffered, and they seek a viable solution. However honest and legitimate their efforts are, it is important that they face reality and not chase the *impossible dream*. As we combat obstacles, we learn how to be mature adults who understand the nature of reality; promises, like balloons, break, plans fall apart, love affairs carry no guarantees, and sacred vows are violated. Everything in life is at least a little bit broken or fragile, unreliable, and tenuous. When a meaningful relationship breaks, pain is inevitable and it is part of the change.

If this is the state of mind you are experiencing, you probably feel rejected, unwanted, and unworthy of someone's love. Loneliness sets into your heart and you feel that *nobody really cares*. Denying this emotion of loneliness can only drive you deeper into isolation. Loneliness is not a sin. Your Creator does not want you to live in this state of mind. I don't believe you like it either. Being that most of us feel vulnerable when we are lonely, it is to your benefit to take time and move forward, calculating each step carefully. Jumping randomly into another relationship, hoping to feel better no matter what the price can be a costly risk. You may discover a better direction if you stop wondering what other people think and who truly cares about you. Focus your attention on yourself—this is not as selfish as it may sound. It is *a good selfishness* because you are making an effort to restore your own image. You were created after the image of God, and that image within you is your soul. If it is tarnished or feels neglected, help it to heal by good thoughts and good feelings about your destiny. Once you begin to feel inner peace, the next step is to reach out and build another healthier relationship. Remember that this other person is also human, so it is good to be cautious. *Make haste slowly* is an old axiom that can be your guide. See how it feels being in the presence of this new person. Do you feel content and encouraged to continue this *new* relationship, or are you trying to fill within yourself the emptiness that loneliness has precipitated? Could this renewed thought, this inner feeling, prompt you to consider your present relationship before you run away?

Humans basically do not completely change; eventually they mature, and this is their choice. *If any change is to take place, it has to start with you:* this is the axiom that I suggest. *But I'm okay. There is nothing wrong with me,* you may say. I reply, *If you really want to relieve yourself of anxiety and destructive stress, then adjust yourself to your situation by renewing your mind.* This is a choice that you can consider.

Adjustment implies a mature approach, finding out who you really are, strengths and weaknesses, and understanding how your relationship with your significant other has evolved. Be aware that both husband and wife contribute to the making or breaking of a relationship. At this point, John F. Kennedy's frequently quoted statement may be modified to suit the occasion: *Do not ask what your relationship can do for you, ask what you can do for your relationship.* Expanding on this statement, I add, *Try not to change your mate; change yourself.*

Chances are you cannot change your mate. You may ask, *Why not? I've changed; I'm a better person. I love my partner.* Some people spend many years of enjoyable married life. Some have children, make plans, and dream about a better life. When one spouse finds reasons to break the relationship, the other who is trying to salvage it suffers more. That partner suffers a departure from the comfort of familiarity and enters into the discomfort of the unknown. The partner feels hopeless and vulnerable. Feelings of sadness, pain, despair, bitterness, anger, regret, and failure often follow. Left behind are fragments of marriage—unfinished business, mixed memories, and loss.

This was the situation with Jane and Chuck. During their seven years of marriage they struggled with the ghosts, traumas, and unresolved conflicts of the past and found themselves on the brink of a break. Scripture speaks of this as the *old self* (Rom 6:6). Negative thinking, fear, guilt, and experiences that would be better off relinquished program the mind of the old self. Realizing that psychological theory and explanations would not be sufficient to help them transcend the hurts of yesterday and their unfinished business, I thought of introducing a spiritual approach. I gave them a CD documentary of St. Paul's life. *He, too, struggled all his life with the old self.* In his First Epistle to the Corinthians 1:30, he says, *"God is the source of your life in Christ Jesus, who became for us wisdom from God...."*

Somehow this verse stood out in their minds, and when they came back to my office, Chuck asked how that thought applied to them. Their inquisitive eyes looked to me for an answer. After a brief pause, I said, *"I understand this verse to mean that God's 'wisdom' is his gift to us. Christ is the wisdom of God, and we can use his teachings to control the emotions that are residuals of our past so they do not become obstacles to our growth."*

In my many years of experience, Jane and Chuck were one of the many couples who suffered from emotional wounds of the past and sought healing. In his book, *The Healing Reminder,* Henri J. M. Nouwen provides words of comfort:

> Remorse is a biting memory, guilt is an accusing memory, hurt leaves a scar, but gratitude of good things that happened is a joyful memory. All negative emotions are deeply influenced by the way we have integrated past events into our way of being in the world. In fact, we perceive our world with our memories.

Herein lies our challenge. Can you and I let go of negative memories that drain our energy, and are we able to select our best memory and use it to move forward? This seems a better choice for a better life.

"What prevented you from making a better choice?" I asked.

"I'm disappointed with Chuck," said Jane. "He's not there for me the way he used to be."

"You are not there for me either," Chuck blurted out. He paused. With obvious sadness in his face, he said, "I'm also disappointed in myself. Things used to be so good between us, and now we don't even listen to each other. As thoughts of divorce and its consequences cross my mind, I realize I have not been a caring person. I'm truly sorry."

"That's why I've locked away my love for you," Jane said. What she did not admit was that she truly cared for Chuck, and locking away her love created greater alienation and suffering for herself. In their individual therapy, I sensed they still loved each other. Divorce could kill love instantly. The only option they could consider was the concept of love. True love means being able to love even in the midst of our most angry times.

When they dated, Jane and Chuck felt strongly attracted to each other. In their romantic state of love, they understood what an intimate relationship could be, and they were aware it was already there. Initially, their married life was rewarding, and both looked forward to being together. Suddenly, in their Garden of Eden, a snake—dissatisfaction—reared its head. But a reservoir of love was still there. Separation or divorce did not seem appealing to either.

This couple chose to continue both individual therapy and joint marital therapy. Individually they dealt with their past hurts. Chuck's mother had died when he was three. He felt rejected by his father's second wife, whom he tried hard to please. She cared only for her two sons. Jane's father was an abusive man, totally unavailable to her. Eventually her mother left him and, taking Jane with her, moved back to her parents' house. Jane grew up with an uncle who repeatedly made sexual advances to her and eventually molested her. Luckily, she found an escape; she entered college and moved into her own apartment. During college years, she met Chuck.

It is evident that both partners of the above-mentioned marriage grew up in dysfunctional families. The love that they felt for each other brought them tremendous relief. However, as they encountered the difficult challenges of married life, memories of painful experiences and harmful early influences of the past came back to haunt them. Their souls were ailing; the relationship suffered. Jane and Chuck's travails were an invitation to open themselves to the sacredness of life. It was time to explore and appreciate what lay ahead, both the known and unknown, the larger truth of who they were and the potential of their life together.

Amid the chaos of confusion and conflict, the perennial questions are raised: *Isn't there some hope? Could my partner possibly change?* Any change requires a will to change, because the character has already been established—any change that a person makes requires the reexamination of thoughts and behavior before sensible changes take place. The only possible hope to improve your relationship depends upon a concerted effort to change.

Marriage is a process involving two complex and ever changing sets of behavior, and, therefore, continuous and perfect harmony in marriage is virtually impossible. It is possible, however, to achieve a useful, livable, and workable relationship. Many marriages are characterized by discord, and yet they survive. To reverse the trend toward destructiveness and make an effort to work as a team requires patience and courage. Most of all, the desire to change is required.

THOUGHTS TO CONSIDER:

- When your faith is strong and you are willing to work hard to realize a noble goal, you stand a good chance of success. *Anything is possible to him or her who believes,* the Bible asserts. If your goal is to change your mate, surrender unconditionally to the process of mature thinking that says, *My mate's attitude may or may not change. It does not have to, but I can adjust to it.*
- Mature thinking is evident when you maintain a positive attitude. Sulking and thinking to yourself, *I'm ill-fated! Look what's happening to me! I can't go on, I don't understand why,* is an insult to you and can cause emotional damage. Such attributes are most destructive and guarantee your downfall. Be aware and avoid this self-pity. Talk to yourself in encouraging and loving terms, and discern what the positive aspects of your life today are. Think peacefully of the positive things that have happened thus far in your life and learn a lesson from each experience.

- What stands between you and what you want from life are merely the will to try and the faith to believe that it is attainable. A belief carries great power because it changes circumstances. When you believe in yourself and in God who is in charge of life, your beliefs will determine the decisions you make and the results that you achieve.
- As a mature adult you don't have to be charismatic or a perfect mate, but you don't have to be arrogant or opinionated either. It is good to be fully human and present, accountable for your life, a contributing member to society, a decent citizen, and a righteous person. Maturity implies moderation and a balanced life with reference to your character, compassion, discernment, understanding, and responsibility.
- Your attitude will directly affect your maturing process and your level of happiness. Developing and preserving an attitude of gratitude will calm your mind, relax your body, and pave the way to a healthier and happier life. Two of the most effective paths that any person can follow to overcome existing anxiety and stress are communicating with your inner self, your spiritual dimension, and connecting with God through constant prayer.

PART II

Sensitive Areas

CHAPTER 9

Facing Disenchantment

When you begin to sense frequent discomfort in the presence of your spouse, you may be asking yourself: "Have I made a mistake to marry him or her?" It may be a normal question. For conscious or unconscious reasons doubt happens to many. Do not be eager to jump to conclusions or make hasty decisions. As you reexamine your thoughts, feelings, and actions, your disenchantment may be of great benefit. It may prove to be an awakening to reality and an opportunity for improvement.

Morrie Schwartz

Disenchantment is a recurrent experience throughout the life of anyone naive enough to believe and trust unconditionally whatever he sees, hears, and touches. As we grow older, we experience many physical, emotional, and intellectual transitions. During our life there will be a long chain of disenchantments, many small and a few large. Sometimes our parents disappoint us, best friends let us down, lovers may prove to be unfaithful, the man or woman with whom we were in love for many years seems petty or dull. Worst of all, when you take an honest look at yourself, you may have to admit disappointment because you are not the person you wanted to be.

The lesson of disenchantment begins with the discovery that some significant part of your past that you once cherished is no longer there. The flawless parent, the idealized mate, the perfect husband or wife, all once believed perfect, suddenly seem flawed. If you bank on ideals, your *inner* self becomes a place of enchantment. Just the thought of an ideal makes you happy.

As long as we sail in smooth weather, most enchantments stay dear to our hearts and make our lives content, but at life's turning points, they are of no comfort. Almost inevitably we feel disappointed at such times. Apparently our earlier enchanted view of life was as real to us as the present point of change. What can we do when disenchantment sets in? Could our turning point be a transition? Perhaps it is the appropriate time to clear our minds from all of yesterday's hurts and ugly memories. We must stop worrying or complaining that life is unfair and start dealing with our present life in a calculated and mature manner.

A mature mind can say, *I am your constant companion and I am completely at your command. I make things happen, successes or failures. I don't want anyone, except God to have power over you or throw you into despair. I'll take charge of your life and look into your background and explore what hinders your joy. When you apply me wisely, I can make the difference. I can help you to move on from the agony of mere survival or maintenance to real joy and progress.*

This is your mind talking to you, and it is the most useful tool that God has given you. No matter how complicated life gets or how difficult your problems may seem, good thinking can make the difference. There is no better way to face disenchantment than with serious and wise thinking. Make it a consistent companion in your life.

When you are facing a major conflict and the words *separation* and *divorce* echo in your ears, you may honestly ask yourself, *Do I really want this person in my life? Is my relationship worth saving, or should I end it?* These are common questions that need sensible and mature answers. Who can really answer these questions, except you? Watch your thoughts, observe your feelings and keep an eye on your behavior.

In critical times, before you run out the door, as many people do, and give up your mate, lover, spouse, or significant other—reevaluate your relationship. Is your situation really as horrible to you as you first thought? It may seem tragic, especially if you find yourself enveloped in a cloud of anger or lingering rage. Suppose you made up your mind: *This is it. I no longer have any feelings for my spouse, and I know why. We were not meant to be together.* If that is the case, nobody can persuade you to change your mind.

The initiative to regain momentum for a better relationship has to start with each mate's individual effort. This may be seen in the case of Lynn and Steven, a couple in their middle thirties who, after nine years of married life, decided to part ways. Although the break happened a few years ago, their experience stands out vividly in my mind. Abusive language and irresponsibility caused an emotional war. They attended marital therapy sessions unsuccessfully. After the third visit, they told themselves that even therapy was going to fail because the conflicts were too painful; their marriage was almost dead. Deep down, Steven loved Lynn and continued with individual psychotherapy. He had gone through a bitter divorce five years before his second marriage, and he began to wonder if there was something wrong with him.

One day at a local bookstore, he was browsing through the section of books about relationships. The title of a book, *Restoring Relationships: Five Things to Try before You Say Goodbye,* attracted his attention. He glanced through the table of contents and the introduction, and decided to buy it. At home, he began to read page after page with increasing interest, underlining passages for rereading.

One night he slept fitfully; each time he woke, he thought about his marriage and wondered if reconciliation was even a remote possibility. He sensed a tinge of hope within—hope mingled with doubt. *Would my wife ever reconsider? She's so angry with me that she doesn't even want to hear my voice. How can I initiate anything?*

Both had already engaged different lawyers. Three months of consultations and twenty-seven thousand dollars later, they decided to give their marriage another chance. Both attended individual and joint marital therapy twice a week. After six months, life took a positive turn, and for reasons of their own, they stopped therapy. Then three months later, I received a letter with a bank check, for the balance they owed me. The letter was one of gratitude, I thought. Part of it read as follows:

Dear Dr. Kalellis,

My husband and I decided to stay together. Something within me that I am unable to explain compelled me to continue trying to be the best I can. Since our last visit, I noticed that our relationship was mellowing, and we both realized how much we love each other. I see my husband now as a different man. I think my attitude has changed. Our relationship is not perfect, but it is workable. We are learning to accept and respect each other and, above all, we are learning to cooperate. We had to stop coming to your office, because we caused a great financial debt; at this time, both lawyers are demanding payment. My husband and I plan to return to therapy soon because we realize that we need to repair emotional damages we have caused, and we need to learn how to deal with feelings of anger when they occur. Steven and I thank you for your understanding and sensitive guidance.

Sincerely, Lynn

Months later, Lynn and Steven came back, and marital therapy continued for another year. They were able to reconstitute their marriage through therapy, commitment, and hard work. Now, five years later, I still receive a Christmas card from them affirming their love.

The above example, although not unique, is evidence of how some people cope positively with difficulties in their relationships. If you happened to be betrayed or bored or disenchanted with your current mate and have serious reasons to break your relationship, you may consider an alternative. Suppose you say to yourself, *I have tried everything to make it work, but our interactions continue to be conflicting. I'm ready to drop the axe.* If you are on the brink of a break, what do you think might happen if you reconsider your decision, as Lynn and Steven did?

If you are willing to reconsider a decision to leave your marriage, say to yourself, *I'll do my part to make it work.* Then, amplify this thought with another one: *I will try to do my part with commitment, courage, dignity, and love.* You may entertain doubts as to whether or not the marriage can be mended and you may ask others for their opinions. However, even well- intentioned friends or relatives may tell you that the marriage is doomed. You have the freedom to tell yourself, *I'm going to try my best.* In other words, make a willful determination to explore and use your own resources to enable yourself to live with inner confidence and peace.

You know some friends or relatives or perhaps one of your own family members who have endured dissolution of their marriage. Most likely, they wrestled with angry feelings, ambivalence, and despair. Functioning at work became difficult, and interaction with associates became tense. Try to think about the unhappiness they felt and the misery they experienced. Do you really want to go through the experience of divorce?

In despair and unable to make a decision, you feel yourself falling apart. At best, you take a path that requires positive thoughts and responsibility for the new choices you will make. Each morning upon awakening, begin to ask questions pertinent to your wellness. *What shall I do today? What could be most important? How can I apply myself creatively? What about my job? My income? Is my home environment clean, warm, and comfortable? What do I need to do to feel appreciated? How shall I deal with my feelings of anxiety, aggression, anger, frustration, failure, or depression?* The questions may be innumerable.

Let's focus on your daily routine: no matter what you do for a living, when logic automatically shifts into gear, you are able to deal with priorities that provide comfortable conditions for you. Meanwhile, let your emotions subside, and you will notice that you are able to move on with more energy to help your own situation.

If you are singularly trying to change a relationship, initially you will face resistance. Your significant other may not believe or even trust your good intentions, sincere as they may be. Avoid the power game and avoid wanting to prove that you are right. Referring to ugly memories of the past does one thing: it poisons the present. In your heart you may know that you are right, but you do not have to prove it. Antagonism or defensiveness cannot work. Simply, they cause distance between people and personal isolation.

THOUGHTS TO CONSIDER:

- If you want to live your life fully and well, learn to embrace opposites. Most likely, your mate may be quite different from you. What makes you think that you can change him or her? Is it fair to negate the personality of another and impose yours so that *you* feel comfortable? Honor your limitations and learn to respect the limitations of your mate. Live in creative tension between his or her limitations in a way that you both fulfill your potential for a better relationship.
- Learn the truth about yourself and listen to the deeper voice within. It speaks the truth about you when you are quiet and your mind is at peace. Meditate on the mystery that you are, fathom the meaning of your life. Becoming your true self takes time. You may have to shake off the old self with its deceptions to discover your new and authentic self.
- Life offers different paths, and you can choose whichever seems most appealing. Be careful of those alluring paths that may be deceiving. They promise glory, wealth, excitement, or pleasure. By now you have the knowledge of your experiences, and if the growth is to continue it needs to be done with measure. Human limitations are subtle. They are of two kinds: limitations of what you are able to do, and limitations imposed by forces outside of you.
- Let go of your attachment to external things or to what is happening to others and become more concerned with what is happening inside your home and within yourself. A marriage cannot survive without mutual care and concern. Avoid negative thoughts and an unloving attitude. Think of yourself as capable of loving. If we do not learn to love and respect our mate, the relationship

is destined to deteriorate. As surely as lack of oxygen will kill us, so will lack of love.

- Try the art of the impossible and walk the steep road that few people take. Silence the outside voices and listen to what your own heart dictates. Avoid the *be good to yourself* theory that claims, *If your mate does not satisfy you, get yourself another one who will make you happier.* It is only a myth that happiness is outside of you and someone else can bring it into your life. In reality, you have no guarantee that life with someone else will make you happy.

- The only person who is going to make a change in your life is you. Be willing to take the first step, no matter how small it is. Learn to love and respect yourself. This may sound selfish. It is not. Can you remember the last time you were in love? It was a wonderful feeling that could only promote healthy behavior. When you love and respect yourself, you are not going to hurt yourself or anyone else, especially the one that you once loved dearly.

- Many of us seem to suffer from lack of self-esteem. As a result, our relationships suffer because we operate on deficits in our personalities. Lack of self-esteem makes us unlovable mates. What makes you unlovable? Your own thoughts: *I'm not worth loving. Why should anyone love me?* The quickest way to change this perception is to start saying, *I am a child of God. I know God loves me.* It may sound simplistic, but I truly believe that in spite of your situation, if you can accept, love, and respect yourself, you will be amazed at how your new attitude will attract love and acceptance from others.

- You can no longer afford to have negative thoughts, judging yourself or your spouse mercilessly. Today is a new day for you. Repeat with the Psalmist, "*This is the day that the Lord has made for me, I shall rejoice and be glad in it*" (Psalm 118:24). This is the moment that you take charge and recreate the life and the relationship that you deserve as a child of God.

CHAPTER 10

Handling Frustrations

Frustration is a prelude to anger. When we don't get what we want when we want it or when we are treated unfairly, instantly we react. If circumstances or external forces prevent us from attaining a desired goal we feel frustrated. Eventually frustration becomes anger.

Charles Stanley

When the hopes and yearnings of the heart do not materialize, we feel frustrated. When our emotional or physical needs are not met effectively, our frustration increases. Often most of us experience this negative emotion as we interact with others. At home, many of us feel frustrated with our spouse or our children or other family members. Each of us has our own different ideas and perceptions about the way things should be. An occasional disappointment with our spouse or frustration at work with a demanding boss or colleague or even a best friend leads to anger and withdrawal.

Now, let's ask a question: *Do frustration or anger serve any purpose other than to cause stress and unhappiness in our life?* Frustration and anger are a waste of time and energy. What if we believed we could make a difference by not reacting angrily, but by responding with understanding and compassion? This belief would make us stronger and more mature. Lack of compassion for the condition and behavior of others precipitates passivity, or worse, frustration and anger.

Caught up in difficult times, we ask for help or we consult others about what we should do; often they give us advice or opinions but not a solution. When nothing seems to work favorably and our frustration is mounting, we should try a new perspective. Start by saying, *This relationship is important to me. I'm capable and willing to pursue it alone.* As the external voices calm down, we may hear our inner voice, the voice of the true self, our soul. This is the new perspective, the potential of our spiritual dimension. When we find ourselves unencumbered by illusive fantasies and external controls, we realize that we have made a better choice.

Life is not a motorized vehicle that we can ride in unencumbered. It is a trail strewn with obstacles. Beyond every obstacle, however, lies opportunity. Sometimes obstacles seem insurmountable. Instead of viewing them as hindrances, we should view them as stepping-stones to help us climb higher and closer to our goals. Beyond any doubt, your goals should include harmony, joy, and peace in your relationship.

Now, let's see if we can apply a similar procedure to your spouse. If you feel frustrated by the relationship, you do have a choice. You may decide to give it another chance or let the relationship die slowly. If you leave things the way they are, gradually whatever is worth salvaging will deteriorate, and the process will be emotionally damaging to both you and your spouse. This may be the time for reevaluation and reconsideration.

The initial steps to approaching your situation may be difficult but not impossible. Facing your mate and having a soul-to-soul dialogue may be stressful. You may have a hard time articulating what is really in your heart or in your mind. Maybe you should simply look at your spouse with a gentle smile and maintain a moment of silence. Listen to your heart pounding. Of course, there is some anxiety in the process. A little anxiety may act as a motivator to help you proceed with kindness and fewer words. Sometimes you may have to go that extra mile of extending yourself because you are aware of possible resistance. This may prove to be a most interesting challenge for you!

As a human being, you may have high expectations of yourself and of others. At times, these expectations may be noble and reasonable. However, if they are selfish and unrealistic—*I know what I want and I want it now*—your relationship will be stressful. The moment you stop making demands on your spouse, your frustration will be reduced instantly and you will feel better. Expect stressful situations as you interact with your spouse. Whatever the tone of his or her voice is, respond with a smile and an attentive ear. It is to your benefit to manage your emotions when you sense conflict. You are in charge of your thoughts. Your thoughts will generate feelings, and feelings will result in action. Take your time.

Ask your mate for help when you feel that your frustration is turning into anger or rage. Say something simple such as, *I really don't want to feel like this. I don't want to be angry with you. Forgive me if I have upset you.* Sometimes it is hard to apologize, but a positive attitude paves the way for calmer communications. If you do not succeed in managing your frustration, it will build up and will control even your best intentions. Then your life will be in a constant state of agitation.

Periodically expressing negative feelings helps alleviate frustration. When you find yourself under a lot of stress, it is important to maintain your composure, asking yourself, *What am I stressed about?* Whatever the source of your stress is, monitor it so you do not unload it on your spouse. Be honest and specific about the nature of your stress without necessarily burdening your spouse with details. Conceivably, you can share personal burdens, but it is wise to prepare your spouse with a disclaimer such as, *I have a personal issue to discuss with you; it is rather heavy. Is now a good time to tell you? I need your opinion.* If the time is appropriate, make sure that you know what your expectations are; do you need advice, opinions, or specific help from your spouse? When your spouse seems favorably receptive, you may say for example, *My mother needs assisted living services, and I don't think she can afford it. I have no idea what can be done about it.* Or, *My brother-in-law, after twenty years of marriage, left my sister for another woman.* Or, *My father had a stroke and he is in the intensive care unit.* If your spouse does not respond in the way you expected, the result may be frustration. If your mate listens sympathetically, show your appreciation. If your information is met with negative criticism or judgment, do not continue the conversation. Carry your own burden and process it carefully. Perhaps you could share personal burdens with a good friend whose response will provide relief for you until you can present the problem to your spouse with a reasonable solution.

If you feel dissatisfied with your spouse and you are not able to maintain a civil dialogue with each other, before you discuss what really bothers you, it would be to your benefit to take time out and process your thoughts and feelings. Do not start with a surprise attack or with an urge to prove how right you are and how wrong your spouse is. If you wish harmony and peace in your home, be careful of your approach. Do not start with a long list of dissatisfactions. Confine your complaints to one area only, be specific, avoid irrelevant details, and stick to the point. Nobody wants to hear a list of complaints; complainers brag about how much they can endure, hoping to evoke sympathy; it is good for you to avoid being a complainer. Aim to resolve the nagging issue in a way that satisfies both you and your spouse. Instead of focusing on negative or angry feelings—how difficult your circumstances are and how your spouse does not really care about how you feel—employ your inner power and take charge of your own life. The divine power within you that keeps you alive—your heart beating, your lungs breathing, and your mind thinking—will provide a new direction. *Get deeper into yourself, and learn from yourself what you must do,* is an ancient axiom that I often quote to my clients. Everything in life has a purpose and a lesson to teach us. As your soul connects with that unimaginable divine energy that moves planets and galaxies and makes the earth go around the sun, this same energy is available to you and will keep you on the trail of life. Be patient. Develop the attitude of looking deeper within and discovering your own God-given strength. Say to yourself, *My expectations have not been met, but I have learned some valuable lessons.* Ask yourself, *Why is it that I expect my spouse to conform to my beliefs and practices? Why should I not allow my spouse to be the person he or she really is, and possibly enable a better relationship?* This approach may promote a wonderful discipline—acceptance of the differences that make life a rewarding experience. Furthermore, couples learn that their expectations should be realistic. Higher, unrealistic expectations invite more frustration.

Another dynamic and effective approach to combat daily frustrations is to ask God to provide wisdom for your situation. He will help you to remove each obstacle that makes your life difficult. Develop and forge your faith that you may understand a God who, in spite of your trying times, is already there for you. Make a decision and persistently connect with your invisible self, your own soul, where God is lovingly present. Believing in his presence, you will not feel alone as you travel on the trail of life. He will provide for you the most effective power—*love*—to face any frustration by loving wisely. Embrace your spouse with love, as Christ embraces you. He will give you the insight to realize that your spouse is not the enemy. The enemy is the devil, the *divider*, who fuels your mind with unloving thoughts, anger, and hate, and prepares you for separation from the person whom, sometime ago, you loved with all your heart and soul.

The following scriptural verse describes eloquently what love is all about:

> Love is patient; love is kind; love is not envious or boastful or arrogant or rude. It does not insist on its own way; it is not irritable or resentful; it does not rejoice in wrongdoing, but rejoices in the truth. It bears all things, believes in all things, endures all things. Love never ends. (1 Cor 13:4–8)

THOUGHTS TO CONSIDER:

- Consciously push the negative feelings of frustration and anger out of your mind and replace them gradually with the good that you see in your mate. Start with positive thoughts such as, *Everything in our relationship has not been bad. My spouse may be facing a personal conflict. I need to be less critical and less demanding. Something special has kept us together thus far; I want to rediscover it and reinforce it.*

- Love can free you from resenting your spouse. Simply, when you let go of a possible hurt that your spouse has caused, your attitude will change. A change in your attitude may help your spouse to communicate with you with better understanding. The question you should ask yourself is, *Do I want to let go of my resentment?*
- Perhaps you need to be a little more giving of yourself. If you model the art of *give and take* in a relationship, life is more rewarding. Good and healthy relationships seldom come naturally. They are a result of strong motivation, careful interaction, and endless practice of good behavior.
- Learn to use obstacles as opportunities to sharpen your skills in order to combat or transcend hindrances. Never give up. Instead of losing perspective and wallowing in deep frustration and self-pity, learn to say no to opposing currents. Before you jump to conclusions, delay action to allow for time to think of the best possible way for you to deal with adversity.
- Try to understand who you really are; respect your true self. You don't have to describe or reveal your true self to anyone. Simply, allow it to surface at its own pace. Once you realize your own value and worth, learn to appreciate your mate. Your self-perception determines how you interact and how you are received by others. Besides physical health, emotional health is necessary if any relationship is to survive and become better.

CHAPTER 11

Anger

Anger is a power for good or evil. It can be channeled and used not only for our mental, physical, emotional health and maturity, but also for the improvement of our intimate relationships.

Martin H. Papovani

Anger is the many-faceted fury that bears directly on our attitude toward life, on our emotional climate, and on our effectiveness as good spouses. Anger often causes physical symptoms that affect our health. Many diseases, including arthritic, gastrointestinal, circulatory, and respiratory disorders can be a result of inverted anger.

Marriage probably generates more anger in the average man or woman than any other social interaction, although many couples manage to suppress angry feelings. Even repressed anger or rage can hurt ourselves as well as others, making us hostile, depressed, and withdrawn.

Uninvited, this unseen enemy enters our interactions at some point and destroys what could be good and beneficial in our life. Most theorists agree that suppressing anger can be destructive to a significant relationship. However, venting anger in its full force can be devastating. Marriage therapists also agree that anger is by far the greatest obstacle in married life. Marriage probably produces more frustration and more anger than any other human relationship in which we find ourselves. If it is not owned and carefully processed, it causes emotional death and victimizes the survivors. Venting anger within limits and with consideration of the other's feelings can be healthy. It is unfair and inappropriate in a loving relationship to hurl one's venom at the intimate other and expect him or her to be lovable and loving in return.

In every marriage there are bound to be times of difficulty when anger causes disagreements and distance between spouses. The longer we wait to take the first step toward reconciliation—to say for example, *I'm sorry that I hurt your feelings; please forgive me*—the harder it will be to restore the relationship.

Anger is a killer. It can rise from circumstances outside of the marriage itself, such as from in-laws, job loss, or from failure to receive recognition or praise. It can rise from inside the marriage as well, such as from the discovery that your partner has been unfaithful. Anger can be the result of sarcastic or hurtful words or as a result of feeling used or unappreciated. It can start from a growing dissatisfaction with yourself: your lack of accomplishment in life, your appearance, your inability to measure up to your neighbors, or your bad luck. What is most important is not where anger originates but what you do with it once you begin to feel it.

Anger may, at times, seem harmless, making us uncomfortably hot or irritable; at other times, uncontrolled, it can be hideously destructive. When you hear a husband or wife exclaim, *Don't touch me. I hate you*, or, *I'm furious with you*, you don't need a dictionary to know that someone is expressing anger. When a hand is raised and ready to strike, it is clear that the person is gripped by rage.

Anger can express itself in less obvious ways. In fact, its disguises can be so subtle—sarcasm or sardonic humor—that when it happens, neither spouse recognizes it. Anger, hate, hostility, rage, resentment, aggression, mental or physical abuse spring from the same source: failure to *get what we want*. This failure provides both spark and fuel for the fire that is easy to ignite in the tinderbox of human emotions.

Constructively channeled, anger can be converted to strength, both physical and mental. Undisciplined and undirected, anger can express itself harmfully. Books have been written about anger and its multidestructive effects; any one of these books may be beneficial reading. Visit your local library.

THOUGHTS TO CONSIDER:

- Anger is a result of your thoughts. Stop being mean, bad-tempered, or vindictive. Harsh words and ugly arguments against your spouse are sabotaging your happiness.
- Be kind to each other, tenderhearted, and forgiving. Forgiveness is a personal action. It is possible to forgive in your heart without ever confronting the one who has hurt you. Silent forgiveness frees the angry person from the bitterness that can be destructive.
- When you don't get what you expect from your spouse, understandably you will be disappointed or angry. These emotions have been part of your life since your birth. We are all born with emotions of anger. They are basically good emotions when justified. They can be of benefit if expressed and dealt with appropriately.
- When marriage does not meet our expectations, understandably we feel disappointed. Realistically speaking, is there any marriage that meets all our expectations? High or unrealistic expectations cause unhappiness. It is wise to examine what we expect from our spouse and be satisfied when some of our expectations are met. We can be mature enough to fulfill unmet expectations ourselves.
- When angry, ask yourself, *What am I angry about? Does my anger serve a purpose?* A wise move would be to distinguish reasonable anger from unreasonable anger. If you care for your marriage, take the first step: express your anger at a proper time, in a proper place, and in an appropriate manner.
- When you repress or suppress anger, eventually you may overreact or even explode. Allow yourself to feel your

90

anger, process it carefully in your mind, and be able to reveal it responsibly. Combine emotion with logic, and use the effective language of humility, love, and tenderness to express it. What if you were the recipient of your spouse's anger?

CHAPTER 12

Jealousy

The symptom of jealousy in all human relationships, including marriage, is so prevalent and so disruptive that we have come to think of it as comparable to an infectious virus—this infection, spread by ignorance and personal insecurities.

Marguerite and Willard Beecher

The feeling of jealousy can generate tragic and insidious effects when it enters a marriage or any other relationship. A husband who jealously notices that his wife praises the virtues of another man feels uncomfortable and allows this jealousy to take possession of his mind. A wife whose husband is eagerly trying to find employment for her own girlfriend may fear that a love affair may develop. Such a wife is setting herself up for a jealous existence. Temptation is always present, but in a healthy and happy marriage, trust can transcend any fear of violation of the vows.

In childhood, jealousy is an emotional state that manifests itself in demands for special affection and attention. With the advent of a younger brother or sister in the family, the older child feels neglected and becomes afraid of being replaced by the newcomer. This type of jealousy is commonly referred to as sibling rivalry. Some parents accept sibling rivalry as normal behavior and expect a child to outgrow it. This is truly a critical period for the older child. Parents need to be sensitive and show equal interest to all their children; playing favorites complicates the situation. Left unnoticed or ignored, jealousy becomes a fixed habit of the mind.

Jealousy is an encompassing emotional condition that engages one person in an impassioned struggle against another. It starts when an individual feels that the other has an advantage—which could be real, imagined, or a condition of life itself. Most people, young and old, are affected by this emotion in varying degrees of intensity and frequency as they compete with and compare themselves to others. Jealous individuals cannot necessarily harm others by their own feelings of jealousy; primarily they hurt themselves. When jealous feelings persist, there is no peace. Jealousy causes relationship problems that can escalate into hatred. According to the Bible, Cain killed Abel in a raging outburst of jealousy.

Since the dawn of history, in most human relationships— marital, family, sibling, friendship, and peer— in the arts and drama and among races and nations, jealousy is present. *I want to have what you have. Where you are, I would like to be.* It is sad to notice jealousy among adults. In most fields of endeavor, this pervasive emotion causes anxiety, anger, and hostility. *Why is she talking to the boss? Why are they always whispering and smiling together? Something must be going on. Recently she's dressed to kill. I notice he's driving a new sports car! Where does he get all that money? I saw them leaving together. Are you invited to her party? Oh no! I'm not among her favorites.*

Jealous people suffer emotionally. Their perceptions become distorted and their thoughts become dark and destructive. Jealousy is associated with lovers' quarrels, so be aware, where jealousy exists, there is no real love, only lust. The jealous person wants to own and control the loved one.

Jealous people tacitly acknowledge their inability to maintain the love of a spouse, and further imply that they are unworthy of affection. The very nature of jealousy is an attempt to control or overshadow the other with our importance, denying the other's freedom of thought, activity, and personal initiative, which are indispensable ingredients for healthy communications and for the preservation of enduring love.

Whether conscious or subconscious, even a tinge of jealousy between spouses can be harmful. Humans are more than what they think and feel; they are more than what they know. It is important when either the husband or the wife becomes aware of jealous feelings; look upon them as seeds under the soil. They have to dissipate and die that they may grow into flowers of admiration and love. This is your marriage. You love each other and you want a happy life.

THOUGHTS TO CONSIDER:

- Most people disclaim possession of such an evil emotion as jealousy. At times they may not be aware that they are possessed by jealousy. If they consider it at all, they deny such feelings: *Me, jealous? What makes you think I'm jealous? I'm fine.*
- Have you ever noticed how jealousy surfaces in sundry forms and fashions among adults? The habit of comparing and competing is so widespread that many people firmly believe that it is a law of nature. Competition, a by-product of jealousy, is often praised as a great and much needed virtue in order to excel in life. Beware!
- Mature, responsible, self-reliant people have little or no need to compete with anyone. They are too self-confident to make jealous comparisons or to blackmail, cheat, destroy, tear down, and torment others in order to rise above them. Mature married couples are too busy and concerned with building a good relationship to allow jealousy into their relationship.
- If you imagine that your happiness depends upon another person or upon other, more favorable conditions and circumstances and you become consumed by jealousy of other people and other things, you are deluding yourself; you are chasing after shadows, for true happiness is a product of a good heart and a pure spirit.

- Analyze the reality of your jealous feelings. They can be emotionally and physically consuming. Realize how detrimental jealousy is to your health, peace of mind, your joyful coexistence with the people who surround you and would support you—and most of all, realize the destruction jealousy causes to your relationship with your spouse.

CHAPTER 13

Other Family Members

Always there is a desire to accept some things and reject others. Who is making this choice and with what wisdom? Does one accept what feels good and reject what does not? Total, complete acceptance is a very real possibility.

Gerald May, MD

Our attempt here is to place our families of origin—namely, in-laws on both sides—in perspective, so you and your spouse may avoid any possible misunderstanding. You have probably heard the old saying, *You can pick your friends, but you can't pick your relatives.* Yet, relatives—in-laws, grandparents, aunts, uncles, nieces, nephews, and stepchildren—are all linked to one another either legally or by blood. You are part of them. They are there by the nature of things, and no amount of wishing will make them go away.

Often, in-laws are the most difficult relationships to incorporate into a marriage. In-law relationships are sensitive, and regardless of how long you have been married, you need to have a viable, even a diplomatic approach in dealing with each other's parents. If you are in the early stages of marriage, your parents may wish to help financially or provide living space for you, or they may give you advice on how to manage difficult aspects of your life. They love to be needed and they take pride in helping their married children. Their own needs for love and appreciation continue years after their grown children leave home.

Sometimes young couples decide to live with the parents of one spouse. This may be for practical purposes—until the son or daughter graduates, until the new home or apartment is ready, or until the newlyweds have earned enough money to enable them to purchase the house they want. Without question, while this sort of arrangement seems practical initially, it eventually causes problems. Parents who extend this type of help tend to set conditions. They want their house to appear in a certain way, they enjoy dinner at a certain time, or they like their furniture arranged in a certain way. When the newlyweds move in, they may have to follow the rules of the hosts. Although you are married, you are a guest in the home of your parents or your in-laws. Should you wish some independence, emotional and otherwise, you had better plan to build your own nest.

Although it is reassuring to know that your parents are supportive of you, it is also important to know that an ongoing support maintains dependency. It could hinder your initiative to establish a strong relationship with your spouse. Life, being what it is, may present obstacles periodically. Your parents may be eager to help you. It makes them feel important in your life. If you are to maintain peace and happiness in your married life, you may have to make a choice. Are you going to seek parental advice, or are you going to discuss marital issues with your spouse?

You may read the Epistle of St. Paul to the Ephesians, chapter 5, verses 20 to 33, which pertains to married life. In part, St. Paul says, *"For this reason, a man will leave his father and mother and be joined to his wife, and the two will become one flesh."* The Christian perspective emphasizes a fact of life: once married, you and your spouse should leave parents behind and move ahead into the newness of your married life. Respect your in-laws, visit them, invite them to your home, celebrate life with them whenever possible, and share the joys and sorrows of the extended family, but in the evening, return to your own nest and take tender loving care of your spouse.

Some parents have a hard time separating emotionally from the young couple. At times they live their lives vicariously through their children. So, some parents are always available. *What a wonderful relationship!* you might say. However, there is a price to pay for such availability: dependency. Moderation may be needed. Parents whose children are married ought to be happy that a new family has started. They can nurture it and support it for a while, but the time comes when the young people need to experience life together on their own and become mature adults separate from their parents.

Parental programming is always present. As you and your spouse enter your bedroom to rest, make love, or go to sleep, two other couples, two sets of parents enter invisibly with you. Parents' perceptions, lifestyle, values, and traditions have formulated your personality; these factors are part of you, although school and society have also contributed to your formation. Instead of ignoring this knowledge, try to be aware of your own character make-up and background to protect yourself and your spouse from trouble.

Of course you might say, *I married my spouse, not my in-laws.* True. However, remember, these are your in-laws, who brought your spouse into this world. They are your relatives and an important part of your spouse. Find ways to integrate them into your new relationship, always remembering that the well-being of your spouse is important.

There may be a time when a set of in-laws needs help. This is a sensitive situation that cannot be ignored. In a good relationship, the couple tries to offer a helping hand in the best possible way. If it happens to be an illness, the son- or daughter-in-law may take turns in helping out. It may be a matter of taking a father- or mother-in-law to the doctor or simply providing a meal. If it is financial help the in-laws need, then the couple has to figure out the amount that they can afford to make available to them. There has to be mutual agreement between the spouses as to how much help they are able to extend to the in-laws to help them over the bad patch. Help should not be considered an obligation. It ought to be an activity of the heart.

Throughout history, all kinds of myths and tales about in-laws have been told. These are often negative comments, usually about the mother-in-law and rarely about the father-in-law, and they should not be taken seriously. I recall a story that I heard some time ago. A young woman entered the seafood market. She looked around and then approached the fishmonger and said,

"I want a fish that is big and has many bones."

"A big fish with many bones?" the fishmonger asked.

"Yes," she said emphatically. "I'm having my mother-in-law for dinner."

Do you respect your in-laws as your spouse's parents? If you do, then you can treat them as real people, sharing opinions, criticisms, doubts, pains, and your love. Maybe it will work the other way around, too; you treat them as real people, and then you may enjoy them more.

If, within these pages, I can get across to you the importance and possible joys of getting to know your in-laws as people, then I will have achieved one of my goals. What often happens is that we meet our in-laws after we have been prejudiced by someone else's opinions of them. It is common, for example, for partners to make statements such as these:

> *Your father is bossy.*
> *Your father is wishy-washy. He's wrapped around your mother's little finger.*
> *I want my mother to baby-sit for our kids.*
> *I don't want your mother to baby-sit my children.*
> *Watch your language when my dad is around.*
> *This is my house, I can talk anyway I want.*

You should realize such statements are negative and may disrupt your relationship with your spouse. If you notice that your in-laws are causing trouble between you and your spouse, reserve the right to your own feelings and personal evaluation of them. If you can see them as people, you can respond to your in-laws as unique and valued persons. They are the people who made your spouse's life possible. You need not adore them; I don't believe they expect adoration. When you have a negative feeling about them, you may take a risk and discuss it with your spouse, but avoid using labels.

Dangerous areas, that in some cases cause divorce, must be mentioned. Perhaps you have heard statements such as the following:

> *My mother-in-law never wanted me to marry her son (or daughter).*
> *My father doesn't like my husband (or wife).*
> *My mother didn't want me to marry my husband (or wife).*
> *My mother cannot stand the woman I married. In her words, "I cannot stomach that woman. You should have married one of those nice girls you brought home."*
> *My father-in-law always wants my husband to do jobs for him. He doesn't realize that his son is now married to me.*

So goes what seems an endless list of complaints about in-laws. If you love your spouse, discover a fresh approach toward your in-laws; at least show respect, for they gave birth to your spouse. Everyone is confronted by the notion that some parents feel, *My son would have been better off if he had married somebody else,* or *My daughter deserves a better husband. My child is good and deserves a better partner.* Destructive results are caused if parents insist on verbalizing their own wishes and ignore the wishes of their children.

A practical step toward a healthy marriage is to learn to respect your in-laws. If either husband or wife has siblings with whom they have good relationships—admiration, constant contact, love—each spouse ought to show proper respect to them as well. Regardless of how difficult they are, accept them for who they are; they have given you your spouse. Invite your spouse to respect your parents or siblings through your own modeling. Do not say, *I have a crazy mother,* or *I have a stupid father,* and expect your partner to respect them. Parents are people, and we need to develop empathy with our partner's feelings toward his or her parents as well as our own.

It is wonderful when couples interact with their parents on an adult level, like friends. When joyful events—birthdays, anniversaries, name days, and major holidays—are celebrated either in the parents' or in the children's home, sensitivity is necessary to balance out the preferences. They should not be confined to the home of one partner's in-laws. If that were to become a tradition, the other partner might complain, *We always go to your parents' home*, and then antagonism and dissatisfaction would set in, causing distance between husband and wife. An easy way to avoid such complaints is to alternate the visits and make it known to both sets of parents. Each of you may still be filled with sweet memories of special traditions in your family. Now you may have to incorporate these with your spouse's traditions as you create new traditions of your own. Team up for the holidays and plan on making them unique. Celebrate holidays in your own home and invite your parents and your in-laws if you wish.

Good marriages become better when spouses recognize the strengths and weaknesses of their parents and place them in perspective. You are now an adult, and you should allow your parents to have their own opinions. Likewise, it is healthy to make known your own preferences. All this does not mean that you don't respect your parents or your in-laws.

THOUGHTS TO CONSIDER:

- It is not your mate's fault for inheriting several characteristics from his or her parents. We are all, to some degree, programmed by our parents and have probably adopted some of their characteristics and habits.
- Consider holding on to values that come from your family of origin that could enhance your married life. This may please your parents and make them proud of you; above all, these values may enrich your marriage.
- Of course in-laws like to be appreciated. Since they made it possible for you to marry their son or daughter, a pleasant climate can be established if each of you discovers ways to show your appreciation. Taking in-laws to a show, treating them to dinner, or purchasing a gift for them will raise their esteem for you and your spouse.

- It can be terribly dangerous and it may cause harm to your marital relationship if you assume a polemic or accusatory attitude toward your in-laws. Not wanting them to visit your home or resisting paying them a visit erects a thick wall between you and them.
- In-laws are part of the marital system. You don't have to feel married to them; simply accept them as they are. Some day your children will need their love. Children love their grandparents, and their love is reciprocated. Eventually your children will get married, and some day *you* will be the in-laws.

CHAPTER 14

Balancing Work and Relationship

Fear of economic failure brings special tensions to a marriage or to any significant relationship. Two paychecks are often required simply to make ends meet since the price of everything is absurdly high and will be higher tomorrow. If the never-enough-money fear is not dealt with sensibly, a couple may be deprived of real intimacy and joy.

John Welwood

The contemporary married lifestyle of most couples requires that both spouses work. The reason does not need much explanation. We need money for the rent or mortgage, insurances, car expenses, furniture, entertainment, and so forth. There is a long list of needs and obligations. Two paychecks are required simply to make ends meet since the price of everything is absurdly high and will be higher tomorrow. Concerns for economic survival bring special tensions to a marriage. If spouses let the economic situation come between them, it becomes a focal point. They overlook each other's emotional needs and attach their energies to concerns over the status of their jobs and discuss what they can do to increase their income.

After having spent a long time climbing up the ladder of career success, Nancy, in her early thirties, decided to get married. During the courting period, Robert was not opposed to the idea of his future wife continuing in her profession. He, too, had a fabulous job with all kinds of benefits such as free travel, health insurance, and long vacations. They considered themselves a lucky pair, both having aspirations of designing a life of prosperity that would allow mutual happiness.

Two years after the marriage, they felt the pressures of their jobs falling heavily upon them. Although a strong emotional bond united them, they felt threatened by the demands put upon their time by their corporations. When they returned home in the evenings, they felt exhausted; they were too tired for companionship, their dialogue declined, lovemaking became mechanical, and eventually they drifted apart emotionally. *What's wrong?* They asked each other, and neither was able to provide an adequate answer.

Nancy and Robert are not the only partners that go through emotional deprivation during the course of married life. Every marriage therapist could produce records showing that two out of three working couples complain about intimacy or their sexual life. While the two incoming salaries pay the bills and provide for material needs, they do not contribute much to intimacy and loving communications. Such couples pay a high price for their stress and fatigue. Each spouse longs for solitude to unwind.

Another stressor that working couples experience is the difficulty they have in appropriating evening and weekend time. Bringing work home, hoping to finish it in the evening or over the weekend, is not good time management. Understandably, in order to catch up or please the boss, some couples convert their homes into a type of workplace. For example, a husband says, *I've brought home a little work.* The wife adds, *I'm all backlogged, and I must work on these papers tonight.* The intention may be good, but is it good for married life? The work takes them away from each other and from those within their household. At times, our work becomes a secret lover that endangers married life. Spouses may identify with their jobs and spend countless hours in the hope of being a success. In the meantime, the marriage is falling apart, for work tends to be a demanding lover and a tough competitor for time. It is not always easy to make the transition from your job to your home, from a tired employee to a responsible, loving mate. When you return home and meet each other after a strenuous day, that initial moment counts for a great deal. It sets the mood for the entire evening.

Nancy, an attractive young woman, received the red-carpet treatment at work and felt fulfilled. Her needs were validated through personal achievement, something uniquely her own. She loved her well-paid job and had real possibilities for advancement. After all, her husband was fulfilled in his work, and they believed their marriage was based on gender equality. At home the atmosphere changed. She came to realize how demanding her schedule was and how unavailable she had become to her husband. In spite of her and Robert's contribution to domestic necessities, she felt she should not be dedicating so much of herself and her time to her job; she knew she had responsibilities to her married life and her home management. This was an additional stressor at home that consumed her time for rest over weekends and holiday breaks. She did have a good sense of interior decorating, and she felt the general appearance of her house, furniture, carpets, curtains, and colors were her job. Robert was cooperative, but interior decorating was not his cup of tea. He admitted his inadequacy and approved of his wife's choice of home decor.

Career couples face many stressors. As they combine career responsibilities with endless domestic obligations, couples may discover that a number of their values are different. These values need clarification, definition, and ownership—*my values, your values, and our values.* People who welcome married life with few boundaries to their values and expectations have a better relationship because their lifestyle allows them the freedom to do essentially what they want. Ultimately, however, they have to define what values are important to them. What are the limits that keep them from total self-absorption? How will each spouse know if he or she is fulfilled? Realistically, can one spouse assume responsibility for total fulfillment of the other, regardless of how much they love each other? However, a reasonable agreement is needed in questions like: *How big should our house be and in what location? What kind of a car will we be happy driving? How much money should be set aside? How hard does each one like to work? Should we practice our religion and become members of a church? Is God a part of our life? How important is our faith? Are we growing spiritually?*

Besides being a partnership, marriage is, in essence, a spiritual relationship. When two people who claim love for each other suddenly begin to feel distance between them, there is a spiritual dimension missing that cannot be brushed aside. Marital therapy and application of psychological principles alone, regardless of how brilliant they sound, cannot provide a lasting solution. Why? Because their souls are suffering and they need to heal. I have listened to heartfelt comments, in counseling hundreds of troubled couples and families: *We would not have made it without help from our church. Faith and consistent prayer has been our salvation.*

In my personal life I have seen people who suffer and find comfort in their faith. Although my knowledge of other religions is limited, I see that people of other than Christian orientation seem to have similar results as they reconsider the importance of their faith. When Leyla, a Muslim who had serious reasons for divorcing her husband, came to me for counseling, I asked her if she had any objection to my being a Christian therapist. She replied, *"I have read a couple of your books, and you seem to carry a spiritual flavor in your writing. That's what I like."* I asked if she practiced her faith, and she said, *"I read the Koran and pray five times a day."* I encouraged her to continue practicing her beliefs, for God's infinite love provides healing for wounds and frequently repairs hopelessly shattered relationships. Sometimes pain and crisis bring us to our senses. There is something about great stress that takes us back in the direction of responsibility.

Remember the biblical story of the prodigal son? When he wasted all of his inheritance and had no money left to buy food, he was reduced to eating from the trough of food intended for the pigs. It was then that he came to his senses and returned to his father. Before he had a chance to apologize and ask for his father's forgiveness and help, his father embraced him, kissed him, and prepared a celebration for his son's return. The message in the prodigal son's story offers a message to couples that feel alienated from God. The once legally approved and blessed marriage may be at risk of divorce if the couple does not confront what is missing in the relationship.

When I hear couples and individuals say, *O my God*, or *Only God knows how I feel*, or shouting *My God* in critical times, I can say, *God does not go away in spite of our attitude or condition.* A client of mine had to face a major tragedy in his family. He claimed to be an agnostic, but at one of our sessions he said, "*I do not know if God exists, but if he does, I want to find him.*" God is ever present in our lives. He makes his presence evident in a conversation with a friend who is a believer, or through a spiritual experience, or in the midst of a tragedy. A lyric in a song or play or a profound look at nature's glory reminds us of his nearness. It is then we realize that the human soul has a deep yearning for God, the ultimate power.

God created marriage, and marriage is the continuation of God's creation of human beings. When people believe that God is the Creator, marriage then is not merely two people in a casual relationship, but three—a husband and wife and God. By failing to address the question of spirituality, the marriage will not achieve the intimacy and growth that God intended. Inviting God into our lives—becoming involved in charity work or in a spiritual activity, going to church, reading the Bible—may not instantly solve marital problems, but it enables us to mature. We realize that we are members of God's world and discover wholeness, a potential in our lives. Our perceptions of what is real and rewarding take a different direction, one that is based on love.

The following are guidelines to trigger a positive tone:

- As the working day comes to an end, slow your pace, if possible. Shift into neutral gear before turning off the engine. Follow a similar pattern in bringing an end to your day's labor. No matter what work you do, as the time approaches to return home, do something simple and get ready to slow down the adrenaline. That's enough work for the day.

- If you have a setback at work and the irritation persists, process it in your head on your way home. Try to dissipate the annoyance before you arrive home. You are not married to your job. While you are driving, listen to soothing music so that undesirable thoughts will be tuned out. If you travel by train or bus, have light or humorous material available to read on your way home.
- When you are a few steps from your door, clear your throat, pull in your stomach, and raise your head. This is your residence, a place where you find peace and rest. Regardless of how you feel, the workday is over. Anything that caused discomfort at work is behind you. You are ready to greet your spouse. Let this greeting be heartfelt, warm, and pleasant.
- If you are truly exhausted and simply cannot function, then it's time to acknowledge this condition to yourself and say to your spouse, I'm going to lie down for a few minutes; I need to close my eyes for a little while, but I'll be with you shortly. This is a better approach than behaving in a grouchy, demanding, or angry manner.
- If you wish to see a difference in your current life, appropriate time for prayer. *I do not know how to pray*, you may say. It matters not. You do not need a new vocabulary. Speak to God as you would speak to a dear friend. Relax, for God is in control. Let him speak to your heart, and words will come to your mind.

Since every problem has a solution, perhaps we ought to seek solutions for career couples who want their marriages to last and work effectively. You want your relationship to blossom, to mature, to reward you to the point where you are able to say, *It's great to be home. I'm glad we're together.* Your time and energy are most valuable. However, they are limited. One cannot channel time and energy in one direction only. Balance is needed. Examine your priorities, your attitudes, and your expectations. Then, when the climate is friendly and conducive to a good conversation, talk about a plan with regard to your careers. Consider the following questions and points:

- How important to you is your relationship?
- What are your expectations in your marriage?
- What changes do you anticipate making in the current year?
- What are your career goals?
- How do these goals affect your marriage?
- Do you consider your job more important than your mate's? If yes, why?
- If one of you makes a career change, how will the other accept the change?
- If one of you makes less money than the other, does it matter? Why? or Why not?
- Admit your personal opinions as your own. Share, but do not make your opinions a problem or impose them on your spouse.
- If illness or pregnancy interrupts the cash flow, how will you deal with less income?

Unquestionably, the above list is not complete. You may add pertinent issues. What is of importance is how you address each issue. Positive attitude and sensitive input could provide desirable solutions.

THOUGHTS TO CONSIDER:

- Respect each other's opinions regardless of whether or not you agree with them. Both of you are entitled to your personal opinions. We are entitled to our opinions, but we do not have to impose them upon others. If your spouse happens to be of a different faith or different cultural background, do not degrade his or her belief system by too much praise of your own faith. Practice what you believe faithfully and encourage your spouse to practice his or her own faith.
- As you honestly express your own needs to your spouse, specify what your expectations are and indicate how he or she could help you meet these needs. Think of your

spouse as your personal friend. If you treat guests or friends with special care and generosity, why not treat your spouse as *the* significant person in your life.

- Be appreciative of each other's careers. Do not underestimate or put down your spouse's job or profession. What each partner has chosen to do is important to that partner. No matter how busy you are, make time for a hug or a kiss or both. A gentle physical touch is reassuring. It shows that you care about your spouse. Is there time in your busy schedule to offer a prayer of gratitude to God for all the good things and opportunities that are available to you? Can you invite your spouse to pray with you?

- When your job or career becomes exceedingly demanding, consider the fact that you have a responsibility to your spouse. Your spouse can be a stimulating component in your life. A happy husband or wife usually carries a good attitude to work. Do not monopolize your time together by talking about your job. Simply, yet briefly, share your daily work experience, your thoughts, your frustrations, your joys, and your plans, and end your talk on a positive note.

CHAPTER 15

Managing Money

Money never made a human being happy yet, nor will it. There is nothing in its nature to produce happiness. The more one has the more one wishes to have. Instead of its filling a vacuum, it makes one. If it satisfies one want, it doubles and triples that want in another way. A true proverb to rely upon is: "Better little with respect of the Lord, than great treasure, and trouble therewith."

Benjamin Franklin

Wealth is a blessing or a curse, depending on the priority it has in your life. It is tragic when the acquiring of great wealth becomes the driving force in a person's life. Whenever money is idolized it destroys everything that is beautiful and worthwhile in terms of character and personality. Attaining a lot of money often causes a person to become self-centered and contemptuous of those who have less.

Money cannot buy love, joy, compassion, peace, or kindness—qualities that are essential for an abundant life. Money helps make life easier when there is an illness or a need to repair some material damage or a desire to fulfill a wish. We need to remember that money can buy books but not intellect, a home but not happiness, luxuries of all kinds but not culture, food but not appetite. It can build a church or temple, but it does not guarantee a place in heaven.

Money issues are rarely discussed before marriage. During the dating period, most prospective mates are generous; they travel to exotic places, eat at expensive restaurants, attend out-of-town events, plays, concerts, and movies. Their lifestyle tends to be extravagant, and each is willing to spend money to impress the other.

Money is often the major contributory factor to marital discord. *He is not making enough. Maybe he should get a second job. She is spending too much on herself. She says we need a new kitchen, but she doesn't even cook. He is always buying gadgets.* Troubled couples tell marriage therapists all kinds of stories, which mean one thing: they are unable to examine and resolve money problems. Such situations need professional help. Often a dispute over money is symptomatic of deeper emotional problems, either individual or shared. Some money problems require education and guidance. Others require therapeutic treatment and deep self-examination.

Couples who would like to remain together with less anxiety need to learn to be sensitive to the way they are spending money. Clever advertising artificially creates wants that, most of the time, have nothing to do with what we really need. Each commercial is designed to convince us that our life will be much easier if we buy the latest gadget, that we will be much happier if we drive an expensive car, that we will make a stunning impression on other people if we use a certain cosmetic or wear a certain garment or belong to a certain club.

Of course, there is instant pleasure in owning certain expensive commodities, but stop and ask yourself: *Does my personal value increase because I drive a particular make of car or because I eat at an elegant restaurant or because I wear designer clothes?* You can see that living on the edge of your resources may cause trouble. Marriage brings expenses—renting an apartment or buying a home, paying numerous bills, including property tax, insurance, yard upkeep, car maintenance, furniture, entertainment, child care, groceries, doctors—the list can go on and on.

Prior to marriage, each one of us had a special attitude about spending money. In married life, money for personal spending has to be cut back, often making partners feel deprived and diminished of freedom. Increases in income don't seem to help the shortage of money because each day presents new wants. In such a state of mind, a partner could easily be jealous of the other's buying habits; he or she could feel cheated; it could lead to the couple competing with each other, with the one who makes more money feeling entitled to spend more. When bills for the household pile up, the couple may take it out on each other in bitter quarrels.

Today we live in an acquisitive society. It is easy to buy items because we want them rather than because we need them. When we are angry, frustrated, or depressed, pulling out a credit card and making a purchase may make us feel powerful and in control of at least one part of our life. Instant satisfaction is what people are accustomed to. But, like a piece of candy that gives you instant energy, spending money because you are angry may give you only temporary pleasure.

A prominent lawyer we will name Bryan, a partner in a prestigious firm in New York City, sought therapy. *"I suffer from depressive bouts,"* he said. *"My associates began to notice. Even my wife complains about my moods."* Divorced twice and married for the third time, he began to question what could be wrong in his life. In view of his success and his wealth, why could he not be happy? Besides his elegant home surrounded with gardens and containing an indoor swimming pool, he also had a house overlooking the ocean and a forty-two-foot boat anchored at his dock.

Beautiful homes, expensive cars, gorgeous clothing and glittering jewelry for his third wife were obviously important attainments for Bryan. They gave him temporary happiness but not a sense of joy or peace of mind. In his pursuit of financial success, his happiness did not increase. He had ignored his three children and his previous two wives. He had no time for friends, but for his clients he would give elaborate dinner parties with live music and dancing. According to the IRS, his annual income was over a million dollars, and his investments in real estate brought substantial profit. He was able to buy several commercial buildings primarily to make more money, but he could not sleep at nights, and his work at the firm had suffered.

A question that lingered in my mind was, what else did Bryan have to sacrifice in order to achieve greater financial success? In studying his lifestyle, the answer came to me. *If we equate happiness with material success, we will never achieve the amount of success necessary to make us happy.* There were healthy reasons for Bryan's pursuit of success. Financial security was important to him. Some of the material trappings of success provided recognition for his accomplishments. He was driven by the attainment of wealth because his parents gave him love only when he got good grades in school or when he scored well in sports. Bryan was highly successful in commercial real estate because his success functioned like a drug: he took it in increasing doses to medicate pain. But *being a workaholic* is unlikely to bring long-term relief. It brought him misery.

The solution lies in a deliberate facing of facts. True happiness and worth are not really bought with money. Life can actually be more pleasant when one is content with simple things. People don't like you better when you compete with them; they are more comfortable with you when you don't threaten them and when you allow them to feel superior. Remember, most of the really worthwhile things in life—the world of nature, the sea, the mountains, sunshine, fresh air, good books, friendship, caring about others, sympathy, understanding, love—can be had at little cost or for nothing! There are several ways that a couple can handle their money together. What works for one couple may not work for another. Amicably discuss with each other methods of dealing with your finances and practice them for a period of time while you develop a plan, a realistic plan, to manage your money effectively. Your money will increase or decrease depending on your plan. Part of your plan should be the establishment of a joint savings account: *our money.* The more capital you put into *our money,* the better you will be able to manage as a team. It will give you a good feeling when accumulating earnings actually becomes fun, allowing you to sit down together and make plans for the use of your joint savings.

Take a notebook and enter your necessary expenses, that is, those that must be paid—taxes, insurances (car, life, health, property, homeowners), interest or payment on debts, and mortgage. Then set aside an amount, ten percent of your combined earnings if possible, for an *emergency fund* to take care of unexpected events such as a broken pipe in the basement, a car repair bill, illness, or the sudden loss of income. This emergency fund should be built up until it is the equivalent of two or three months' income, and then maintained at that level. Estimate day-to-day expenses: shelter, food, clothing, contributions, gifts, transportation, and recreation. This type of budgeting may vary, but the more skillful you become, the better you will be able to stretch dollars to make the difference between feeling comfortable and feeling pinched. What should not be overlooked is the setting aside of money for personal allowances, which each of you may spend without being challenged.

There are many ways of handling finances. If a relationship is sound, a couple may work out a reasonable approach that will also enhance their communication. It is of relatively little importance whether the husband or the wife undertakes the general management of the checking account. This usually depends on which one is the more efficient with numbers and management and is willing to assume the responsibility of balancing the checkbook.

However, it is important to stress the difference between normal and neurotic approaches to money. In a normal situation, money is a means to an end. Normal couples are careful not to allow themselves to be taken advantage of in money matters. For example, when a salesperson knocks on your door or appears on television and makes a persuasive pitch for a product, it is important not to be seduced and spend money on something that you had no intention of buying. Make the distinction between the two questions: *Do I need this? Do I want this?* I need air to breathe. I need food to sustain myself. I need my car to drive to work. But do I need a super vacuum cleaner to clean my one-bedroom apartment?

Some couples set goals and, based upon what seems to be their priorities, they make plans. Here is an exercise you might find of interest. Pretend that you have $50,000. What would you do with all or part of that money? Travel? Buy a boat? Put a down payment on a house? Buy needed furniture? Start your own business? Help relatives? Donate to charitable projects? Pay bills? Invest in stocks and bonds? Reserve money for the education of children? Go back to school for further education? Buy another car? Buy a new computer? Your list may be longer than you thought. Answer the above questions individually. Then get back together and discuss your individual responses. Compare your answers. Discover your common interests and goals with regard to money as well as the differences in money management styles.

Some couples find it practical to budget a percentage of their income for their various expenses. You know what your general income is, and a workable breakdown may be similar to the following:

Housing: 26%
Food: 15%
Credit: 13%
Personal: 8%
Savings: 8%
Clothing: 7%
Transportation: 7%
Utilities: 4%
Recreation: 4%
Insurance: 3%
Miscellaneous: 3%
Furnishings: 2%

Whatever plan you choose, it is important that you and your spouse agree on the choice. Should this choice not seem as practical for you, try not to blame your partner. A *you-made-me-do-it* mentality can be emotionally disturbing. Instead, make another choice, possibly a better one, together.

Money can be a blessing and should be interesting to deal with; you ought to be able to manage it rather than having it manage you. How can you save enough to be able to make good choices for it? How can you avoid worrying about it?

THOUGHTS TO COI

In a society of experts, someone   you
with your finances. Many marriag   ally
because of poor planning. Before
anyone, remember the following po

- If both spouses are working an
  are you satisfied with the way
  both incomes? If not, meet with a
  sultant who can explain ways to ma
- Some financial experts are better tha
  few and see which one seems to unders
  best. Observe your feelings during the
  if you are connecting with someone that y
- Some consultants have pet projects or inve
  that they push. Exaggerated talk about peop
  helped may sound very convincing. Keep in n
  investors make a hefty commission when you
  their projects.
- Deal with reputable firms. Investments have risk
  risk of loss and the prospect of gain are always pres
  Learn about investments through research. You sho
  gain knowledge of their operations, net profits, commi
  sions, and financial positions.
- When investment offerings are made over the phone, as
  appealing as they may be, be skeptical. Beware of urgent
  appeals promising spectacular returns. Obtain further
  information from the Better Business Bureau or your
  state securities commission before committing to an
  opportunity.
- When you talk to a certified financial planner, make sure
  you understand the services that will be provided, how
  often you will consult together, and a breakdown of the
  fees and charges involved. Make sure you get a written
  copy of what the planner has offered.

PART III

Sources of Strength

CHAPTER 16

What Is Love?

O Lord, look with favor on us, and impart Your love to us—not as an idea or concept, but as a lived experience. We can only love each other because You have loved us first. We can see that all human love is a reflection of a greater love, a love without conditions and limitations. In hidden ways this love sings a song in every human heart and plays a role in the history of the world.

Henri Nouwen

When we raise the question *What is love?* it is like asking, *What is God?* Our finite minds cannot easily define love. All descriptions of love by poets, wise teachers, and sages tend to be inadequate, for love is the essence of life, and life itself is a mystery. There are many other mysterious elements in our life that we do not understand. We do not see or touch electricity or the air we breathe, and yet we know they exist, for we enjoy their presence. What, then, is that magnetic power that attracts us to one particular person among a hundred others and makes us feel that we have found the greatest treasure in life?

People who are genuinely attracted to each other and want to have a lifetime relationship experience this powerful feeling called love. Lovers, overly enthusiastic or under a spell, may express themselves in the following ways: *I'm crazy about you. I love you so much you drive me crazy. Even hearing your voice over the*

121

phone makes my heart jump. Baby, you've got everything that I need. I want to be with you forever.

Songwriters, movie producers, and novelists exaggerate and expound creatively on this theme to the point of convincing thirsty hearts that the only thing a human being needs is love. *All I want is love!* Of course, without love we die. Love implies responsible action, respect, and caring. Have you ever been in love? I mean *really* in love. Do you remember what it was like at the beginning? The joy! The excitement! The anticipation of being with that special person! Close your eyes for a moment and think of that period of your life. This was your experience of *being in love.* Love with all its ramifications is a decision.

We are born to be loving people. I want to be loving and you want to be loving. Our relationship can be loving. A person decides to love another and to be *lovable.* Most of us know of mother love, father love, sibling love, love of a friend, love of country, and sexual love. The Greeks have more than one word for the different kinds of love that we experience:

Agape: Agape is a nonpossessive, nondemanding, nonjudgmental power that helps and allows the partner to grow according to his or her own natural bent. It arises out of a feeling of self-sufficiency and wholeness, not out of a feeling of emptiness. It is the deep, rich love of good friends, a loving feeling with neither a sexual nor a filial component.

People who truly love aspire toward realistic goals that bring joy and fulfillment in their relationships. Marriage and family therapists and psychotherapists often speak of the powerful forces that bind people together in love. Religious leaders speak of the manner in which God loves us and of proper ways to love God. "...*love the Lord your God with all your heart,...all your soul,...all your mind, and with all your strength*" (Mark 12:29–30).

Eros: Eros is a possessive feeling, a manipulative, acquisitive form of desire. It is the sexual erotic love of man and woman that, if used with sensitivity, enriches their life together. It is destructive when sexual love aims to control or subjugate the other person, using him or her to serve individual needs. People in a state of eros live a life of ecstatic inertia, sometimes enslaving their partners whom they purport to love. Eros involves the feeling described in the words, *I can't live without you*, or *If you ever stop loving me and leave me for somebody else, I'll die.* This implies a low self-image of the supposed lover and a deeper need to create dependency and foster manipulation.

Philia: Philia is a feeling of wanting to be with someone to share an experience, personal issues, happy or sad events, future aspirations, and information—provided that this feeling is reciprocal. Unlike the relationship of acquaintances, philia love is a form of an unwritten contract entered into by two people pleased to be with each other. Real philia love is a kind of divine act that enables two people to share thoughts and feelings that life denies them. It is the concept of friendship that requires a mutual contribution of loving exchanges and trust. It cannot be sustained unless they both invest time to be present in each other's life. In good times joy is enhanced; in troubled times philia can be therapeutic. When philia love is present in a marriage, God has bestowed upon those spouses the ultimate bliss.

Philanthropia: Philanthrophia is a feeling of caring for the *anthropos,* the human being—a concern about another person and his or her well-being. In everyday life, it can be a positive force that enables us to give part of ourselves—time, emotional or financial help, a kind word or a smile to another person, even to a stranger. Another word for this is *charity*; this is a term often used as an expression of unselfish caring or help for institutions that promote the welfare of the community. History has given us numerous stories of philanthropists who have given selflessly—talent, money, food, medicine, and survival material—to charitable institutions and war or natural disaster victims.

Storge: Storge is a feeling that a mother experiences when feeding her infant, not when the little baby is crying because he or she is hungry, but because she feels the milk overflowing from her breast. It is the ability to show a feeling of tenderness and warmth, not only to helpless children but also to all those whom we love, whether friends or relatives. Learning how to show storge—affectionate love—implies that we become sensitive to two things:

1. How the other person wishes to receive this type of storge love and how appropriate it is to extend it to him or to her.

2. When to show this love. You need to know the appropriate time and degree for expressing a loving feeling, when to take the initiative, and when to hold back.

In harmonizing all of the above aspects of love, as the conductor of a concert harmonizes a number of different musical instruments to produce melody, each of us can gain a driving force that encourages us to focus our attentions on each other. Love inspires us to know and understand the people we have brought into our lives. It gives us each the insight to see, appreciate, and accept our spouse, without a desire to change him or her to match our personal expectations.

St. Paul's First Epistle to the Corinthians, speaks of love:

> If I speak in the tongues of mortals and of angels, but do not have love, I am a noisy gong or a clanging cymbal. And if I have prophetic powers, and understand all mysteries and all knowledge, and if I have all faith, so as to remove mountains, but do not have love, I am nothing. If I give away all my possessions, and if I hand over my body...but do not have love, I gain nothing.
>
> Love is patient, love is kind, love is not envious or boastful or arrogant or rude. It does not insist on its own way; it is not irritable or resentful; it does not rejoice in wrongdoing, but rejoices in the truth. It bears all things, believes all things, hopes all things, endures all things. Love never ends. (1 Cor 13:1–8)

Beyond any doubt, the presence of love makes a person more attractive, more pleasant to be around, and a joy to work with and for. Lovable people make better marriages, have good parent-child relations, meaningful friendships, and a satisfying life. Truly, it is a challenge to be a lovable person; however, the effort to be lovable is rewarding, for it builds character and endures adversity.

What does this challenge, this ability to love, involve within a marriage? It requires the simple effort of doing something for your mate even when you don't have the desire to do it or the time to do it or when you would prefer to do something for yourself instead. You need to be cooperative and patient and treat your mate with kindness and respect regardless of the circumstances or your own needs.

Love is a feeling that may initiate a marriage, but the cultivation of love is what sustains it. Bring a beautiful plant into your home. Leave it alone and it will die. Give it water and nourishment, prune it, expose it to air and sunlight and the plant will thrive, beautifying its surroundings. Love is like a plant. If it does not receive proper nourishment and care it will die. Love needs daily nurturing. Mutual concern and respect for each other flourish only if the couple understands that love cannot be taken for granted. Nurturing does not mean, however, that the couple should be in full embrace all the time. *"Let there be spaces in your togetherness,"* says Khalil Gibran in his book, *The Prophet.*

You need to realize you are part of a couple and not leading a single life. Spend personal time to please your mate, even when you are dealing with a busy schedule. Be honest and just, compassionate, understanding, and tender. Treat your spouse the way you treat a friend. Be more than a gift-giver or sentimental card-sender. Do not get grouchy or upset when times are difficult. Watch the degree of your irritability when you are faced with a totally personal problem. Process your feelings before you reveal them to your mate. Don't take your frustrations out on her or him. You may speak about the problem or share your concern without expecting your spouse to provide a solution.

If your spouse is facing a serious personal problem, listen attentively but don't rush to give advice or to say you should or should not do this or that, or *I told you so, but you never listen to me.* Love implies that you are patient and supportive during difficult times and during misfortune.

Find joy and love in your faith. Believe in God who brought you together; he is not going to let you down. Marital happiness is a by-product of a loving cooperation and mutually creative and productive life. Marriage is a source of happiness when you have a loving relationship with your spouse as well as companionship, support, and mutual goals. A wonderful thing you can do in your marriage is to share the interests and thoughts that you have that are different from your mate's. Revealing differences may cause conflicts. Conflicts show us our imperfection and uniqueness. You cannot expect your mate to agree with you all the time. Conflicts are an inevitable part of married life or of two people living together. Conflicts give us an opportunity to expand our relationship, learn from each other, and become more understanding of the human character.

If you grew up in an unhappy environment, do not bring an unhappy attitude into your marriage. If you have been an unhappy person before marriage, chances are that you are not going to be happy being married. Your significant other will not be able to guess why you are unhappy unless you share this part of yourself openly.

If you are a rejected person, you probably entered marriage starved for love and acceptance. If you have married a rejected person, you married a starving person. If both of you are rejected people, watch out! Your expectations of each other will lead you to heights of frustration, anger, and disappointment.

If a critical father or mother constantly censured you as a child and you internalized that critical voice, then criticism can be your style of handling anything and everything in your life. Make a concerted effort not to bring a critical attitude into your marriage. No spouse can be comfortable being criticized, even if your intentions are good.

If you constantly question your partner's love, real trouble is on the horizon. After a while the partner will become fed up with your doubting attitude and say, *You can believe what you want to believe. Either you accept what I say or you don't. I don't know of any other way to convince you that I love you.* A response like that reflects frustration, and the doubting person feels more rejected. All this amounts to one thing. Those who were happy while they were single stand a good chance of being happy in their married lives. Others will have to work a bit harder to achieve this happiness. Marriage is a mystery. Enjoy it with a good attitude, live it with faith, and support it with love.

THOUGHTS TO CONSIDER:

- Love is an evolutionary process, starting as a flame and gradually becoming slow-burning embers. Love requires care and work by both partners to maintain the energy of the fire, and this care and work should become habitual if love is to thrive and grow. In reality, love is action, especially after the emotional high of infatuation has subsided. In the best of circumstances, love is always a work in progress.

- Strong opinions about virtually everything, including each other's behavior, result in quarrels, hard-to-solve conflicts, and inevitable anger. These destroy loving feelings. It takes less energy to think in positive and productive terms: *I want to love you when times are good and bad. I want you to love me even if I am upset. Let's agree to love and respect each other even when we disagree. I want to be loving and lovable.*

- In the middle of a marital crisis, when anger and impulse dart across your brain, you might say, *This marriage is not going to work. I may as well pack my bags and walk away.* Are you sure that is what you want to do? If so, a lawyer will always be available to hear your complaints. You could exaggerate them to dispel your anger. A retainer of a few thousand dollars will be requested, and you will be on your way to a divorce. It is less expensive to meet your challenge with courage and face your spouse with a better attitude: *I love you. I will always love you, and I want to find a way to work with you.*

- Love can be a source of great joy when there are no strings attached to the loving process. This means that when we show love to our spouse, we should not do it for selfish motives. When a couple respects each other's personality and well-being, when they share responsibilities and are interested in each other's happiness, there is healthy love. A love that is lasting is spontaneous and comes from within; it must be maintained and reinforced, otherwise it fades and dies.

- A demonstration of real love is more than an offering of beautiful flowers, generous gifts, and sweet words, and more than candlelight dinners or moonlight walks. Real love recognizes that the one we love is a human being. We show compassion and understanding during disagreement and difficult times.

CHAPTER 17

Intimacy

Everyone needs a relationship with another person who accepts him or her unconditionally. I love you "just the way you are." The irony is that it does not take long after the honeymoon to discover that the closer one moves toward one's mate, the greater the risk of rejection. This delicate pull-push dance is called intimacy.

Dennis and Barbara Rainey

Intimacy is a significant aspect of love. Genuinely loving a person encourages intimacy. Greater emphasis has been given to intimacy in recent decades, and a plethora of articles and books have been written about it. In a significant relationship, especially in a good marriage, intimacy is not only desirable, it is necessary for the enrichment of married life. Because of its nature, intimacy consists of feelings, thoughts, loving interaction, and physical touch. Each person or each couple perceives intimacy differently. It needs to be understood and practiced realistically, For example, it cannot be a symbiotic existence, as in that of a mother and a child. When intimacy becomes dependency—*You've got to take care of me, baby, because I love you. Or I want you to be near me all the time*—the relationship becomes bondage. One spouse cannot expect the other spouse to be the total source of fulfillment and happiness. Such an expectation could easily cause trouble.

When my children were younger, I used to tell them the story of Sylvia and Larry. They lived miles apart from each other. Sylvia was a gorgeous rattlesnake with silvery skin that shone in the sun. She lived at the top of a mountain overlooking the sea and twisted around a rock, daily enjoying the fresh air while her eyes searched for food. One day she thought, *I would love to eat some juicy seafood.* It did not take long for Sylvia to crawl along the seashore. There she met an unusually strange creature, a huge lobster, basking in the sunshine.

"Good morning," she said sweetly and crawled toward the lobster. "My name is Sylvia; what's yours?"

"I'm Larry," said the lobster.

"You're so handsome, and I'm so happy to meet you," said Sylvia, and slithered close to Larry, tickling him with the tip of her tail.

Larry giggled.

"Can we be friends? I'm tired living alone on the arid mountain," said Sylvia.

"Of course," said Larry. "I'm very lonely too, and I do want to have a friend like you." He leaned gently against the snake. "You are so soft, so friendly and warm."

Meanwhile, the snake wrapped herself around the lobster.

"We were meant to be together. I always wanted to live by the sea," said Sylvia. "I want to be your friend forever."

The lobster felt rather warm and eagerly asked, "Would you like to come swimming with me?"

"Swimming? Surely, but let's stay by the shore a bit longer; I'm a little tired." Sylvia yawned and twisted and wound herself from head to tail around the lobster.

The lobster could hardly breathe. "You are squeezing me too hard."

"But I like you a lot. I want to get closer and closer to you."

"I like you too," the lobster said, "but you are choking me and I can hardly breathe."

As Sylvia squeezed the lobster tighter, his shell cracked. "I love you very much and I want to be with you forever," said Sylvia.

In agony and utter despair, the lobster, using both his claws, gave the snake a pinch, cutting her into three pieces.

"Now look what have you done to me! Why have you treated me so cruelly?" cried the snake.

"I love you so much. I want more of you," said the lobster. As the snake squirmed away in three different directions, the lobster grabbed one piece and crawled into the sea.

When intimacy is so intense, and one spouse clings to the other and allows no breathing space, the relationship suffers immensely. The clinging spouse absorbs the other, leaving him or her with no personal identity. The best suggestion for a lasting and productive intimacy is the advice that the poet Kahlil Gibran gives us: "*Let there be spaces in your togetherness.*" In spite of their degree of love, spouses need to give each other time and space alone. Some solitude gives spouses time to think, to plan, and to nurture their souls. This enables them to come back to each other refreshed, revitalized, and more loving.

Webster's *New World Dictionary of the American Language* defines intimacy as:

1. "...inmost, most inward feeling;"
2. "...most private or personal;"
3. "...closely acquainted or associated."

Webster's offers a secondary definition of *intimacy*: "*...an intimate act, especially illicit sexual intercourse; a euphemism.*"

People who wish to have an intimate relationship need to be aware of each other's personality—strengths and weaknesses, virtues and flaws; they must have the ability to see the other as a human being and connect in a creative manner that offers a presence of emotional and physical closeness. The word *intimacy* is often used as a synonym or euphemism for *sexual intercourse*. Mass media interprets intimacy as closeness; sex equals closeness; therefore, sex equals intimacy. This is not correct. Such a false syllogism tempts many people to use sex as a shortcut to intimacy. They are misled into thinking that sex is the way to achieve intimacy. In reality, excessive emphasis on sexuality may evoke negative feelings—performance anxiety, impotence, decreased degree or frequency of sexual pleasure—and may cause distance and avoidance. Most sexual malfunctions are a result of emotional conflicts. *Intimacy, sex, love* are intriguing words. To improve marital interaction, spouses need to learn the true meaning of the word *intimacy* and pursue ways to enhance it.

The capacity for love is innate in all of us, but if it is to emerge in its true beauty, its facets need to be successfully cut and polished. It is to be hoped this is what life experiences will do for us. In infancy and early childhood, the facets of love are few and simple and relate primarily to feelings for and from the parents. As we grow older and move outward in our relationships, an even greater number of facets must be cut and refined to achieve the capacity to love that is unique to everyone.

Casual definitions of intimacy reveal how little thought has been given to a word that is even more fundamental, more directly applicable to many human states than the word *love*. Is it possible to feel love for someone without being intimate? Yes! Admiration? Yes! Affection? Yes! Sexual desire? Yes! All of these are possible without intimacy, and all have been falsely equated with love. Physical closeness is not necessarily what is meant by intimacy, either.

Intimacy is a state of being with another, a genuine friendship much desired in life, that encourages and strengthens human relationships. Intimacy is not simply a romantic experience. As we explore the whole concept of intimacy, we become aware of its limitations. Faulty communications, immature behavior, offensive personality characteristics can bring a sad end to what could be a good and intimate relationship. What also seems to cause distance or even a break is the fact that humans are not perfect. As we share our inner life, personal secrets, thoughts and feelings, we become vulnerable. The other person knows everything about us, including our imperfections, and we feel transparent. If transparency is missing, however, the deep desires for emotional and physical intimacy will not be met. Without both intimacy and transparency, trust will not develop. Transparency begins with a firm commitment to create a safe environment for total openness. In 1 John 4:18, we are given good advice: "*There is no fear in love; but perfect love casts out fear, for fear has to do with punishment, and whoever fears has not reached perfection in love.*"

Sometimes intimacy causes anguish and emotional pain. As we think about the person with whom we will become intimate, we fear exposure. Unwittingly or overenthusiastically, we share our inner core, revealing undesirable parts of our self, our blunders, our guilt, our stupidity, and our foolishness, and as a result our self-esteem and the esteem others have for us diminishes. Fear of being hurt or abandoned by the intimate other increases. Does this mean that we cannot be intimate? Of course we can, when we do not take intimacy lightly.

Schopenhauer's fable of the freezing porcupines illustrates difficulties and limits in intimate relationships. Every time porcupines huddle together for warmth or to copulate, they hurt each other with their quills. When they need to be closer together, mutual irritation begins anew. So the porcupines are continually driven together and forced apart. Humans have a similar tendency. Once they feel attracted to someone and want to be closer to that person, the *good feeling* known as intimacy becomes fragile. External or internal forces, or overt or subtle expectations interfere, and intimacy suffers.

True intimacy is basic to love and marriage. How can we attain it? There are two basic requirements: time and privacy. They allow the development of the components of intimacy: *choice, mutuality, reciprocity, trust, and delight.*

Mutuality and reciprocity cannot succeed without trust. Trust, like love, can be developed only mutually. The spouse who trusts a difficult or unloving partner usually is a frightened person, not a trusting one. For people whose trust has been shaken, I suggest a simple prayer like the following:

> God, our Heavenly Father, Lord of the Universe and of our lives, we have agreed to form a marital bond for mutual benefit and happiness. We are aware of our human frailty, yet we hope and pray to accept each other, to change and grow as the years unfold. We realize that neither of us is perfect. We are not afraid to admit that we are fallible and frequently make mistakes. We need your help and direction, dear Lord our God, to be honest and open to each other and to

share our feelings as they occur in the spirit of love. If what happens is joyful we will cherish it. If it is painful or difficult we will accept it without asking whose fault it is, but with patience and tolerance. When we feel frustrated or angry, instead of becoming punitive and destructive, we will make an effort to be consoling and encouraging. We will examine our conflict and resolve it realistically. Instead of deciding who is right and who is wrong, we will devote our energy and intelligence toward a viable solution. Amen.

During difficult times of stress, blurred communication, and crisis, trust may diminish. If, after every crisis comes wisdom, a difficult experience will increase our trust in each other if we have handled the situation skillfully. Trust grows out of shared experiences. It is naïve to believe that in marriage life is smooth sailing. Trust in marriage does not mean, *I am sure, my sweet darling, that you will be exactly the same as I believed you were the day I married you.* Trust is effectively attained when two spouses sustain a flexible, enduring relationship that is able to accommodate changes, storms, transitions, and growth. The steps taken by two people toward trust involve many small revelations, as each one carefully opens the innermost self to the other and tests the safety of that step. Like the sculptor building up his work with tiny bits of clay, spouses gradually build trust and emotional security, and that serves to build up intimacy to its ultimate expression, open *delight* in each other's presence.

In married life, what then does it all mean? Intimacy is a way to attain a sense of oneself, wholeness, a feeling of completeness. It is an awareness and acceptance of who we really are and an existence in harmony with our inner self. We cannot be intimate with anyone unless we are content with our own personality; we must feel good about who we are and have genuine motives for what we do. Intimacy implies uniting with someone else and becoming a part of a meaningful relationship that fulfills a purpose. In addition to the concept of creative coexistence, of emotional fusion and fulfillment, bodily contact is essential if intimacy is to be complete. It is a great attribute that

134

can enrich married life, and it makes married life lasting. It begins as you entrust yourself and your married life to God. He loves you and gave you your mate, so take a deep breath and begin sharing yourself with your spouse at the risk of being vulnerable. The Raineys suggest that intimacy includes your ability and willingness to share the following aspects of yourself:

- *Thoughts.* What do you really think? In a marriage there should be little holding back of what each person thinks and feels deeply.
- *Feelings.* How have experiences affected you? Are you sad, angry, depressed, happy, hurt, or discouraged?
- *Needs.* Are you willing to say what you really need: I'm missing being close to you? I would like it if we made love tonight.

It may appear difficult to communicate deep feelings to your spouse. Do you think that your spouse will perceive you as needy, selfish, or weak? To transcend your hesitation, please review the following plan:

1. Determine *what* you want to say and how important it is to you. Prepare your thoughts ahead of time; outline in your mind, in specific terms, *what* exactly you want to convey to your spouse and why.
2. Think carefully about how you want to say it. What emotions do you want to show that will convey your message—joy, sadness, concern about your spouse and your life together, excitement, or passion?
3. Figure out the appropriate *time* when your spouse is emotionally available to listen to you. Timing is very important. Before sharing anything, observe your own moods, needs, and disposition.

Intimacy begins with a joint and sincere commitment to create a loving climate, an atmosphere where it feels safe to be open.

THOUGHTS TO CONSIDER:

- Assuming that we ever achieve the state of grace we call intimacy, we are caught on the horns of an interesting dilemma. As soon as we have established a mature intimacy based on inner freedom and the ability to share our inner self, we immediately find ourselves confronted with all the seductions of dependency. We would like the other to love us unconditionally.

- Whichever route we take, we cannot begin to get close to others without getting dangerously close to a regressed state in which we abdicate our independence and our capacity to operate as an individual. We say in effect, *Bless me and make me well*, or, *I love you. Take care of me.* The paradox is that we can only become close when we are free of the need to be close.

- As mature adults, we cannot expect unconditional love. Adult love is never unconditional. Seeking such love is a vestige of childhood. Young children need, deserve, and want unconditional love. But when adults seek unconditional love, all they get is disappointment. At best, spouses should need the love of each other, which is not the same as the love we should have received as children from our parents. While we deserve a decent attitude and well-mannered behavior from our spouse, we have first to earn their respect and love.

- A relationship that denies the existence of disagreement, judgment, pain, and anxiety is not necessarily intimate. It is a fantasy that at some point in life intimacy will be good to us, reward us for long hours of hard work, self-sacrifice, and suffering with that warm breast that will hold us affectionately. Such a fantasy may eventually discover that the breast has dried up. Mature people embrace their relationship with all its advantages and limitations.

- This is the ultimate definition of the word *intimacy: two people who delight each other and delight in each other in an atmosphere of security based on mutuality, reciprocity, and trust.* When two people say to each other without words—*I delight in you as a whole person and you delight in me. I can, I want to, I may express this delight in many different ways—* then intimacy is present.

CHAPTER 18

Choice and Commitment

Marriage was not designed to make its partners happy.
It was designed by God for procreation. What brings
happiness into married life is the quality of contribution that spouses make toward their relationship.

Willard Beecher

Millions are the wonders of life, but nothing can be more wonderful than a good marriage. It is one of the most complex systems ever discovered by human beings. In spite of its multiple
complications, it continues to be the most wonderful and
rewarding institution available. Two people fall in love and
under the spell of exuberance, they marry. Naïvely they make a
lifelong commitment to a monogamous union as a viable solution to loneliness, as the most fertile ground to sow and cultivate
the seeds of love. Truly, it is a desirable relationship for mutual
support, respect, growth, and personal freedom. Our life is not
as satisfying as it could be in a genuine relationship that promises fulfillment with each other, regardless of how accomplished
and successful each is socially, professionally, or financially.

Considering the potential good in a marital relationship,
why is it that we have so many unhappily married people? The
present-day divorce rate and the daily turbulence that exists
between some partners who, for practical reasons prefer to stay
married, cannot be ignored. We need viable solutions.

Is there any marriage or relationship that is perfect?

Choice and Commitment

How many times have I heard this question in my past thirty-five years of practicing marital therapy! With a smile and raised eyebrows, I reply, "Mine." Of course I allow my surprised clients to see that I'm only teasing. Honestly, I have not seen a perfect marriage yet. Assuming that we come from an imperfect family, grow and live in an imperfect world that is inhabited by imperfect people, the institution of marriage is imperfect. Even the most loving relationships have their ups and downs; what keeps a marriage going is the partners' commitment. We often hear the word *commitment*; what does it mean? Commitment is an official pledge, a state of being emotionally and legally bound to a course of action. In marriage, commitment implies that a man and woman join each other for life—to continue the journey of married life with all its rewards and challenges. We must understand that commitment alone is only part of the equation for a good marriage. Commitment must lead to a skillful development of healthy communication, accountability, respect, and wise choices that make a better marriage. As you read these lines, think about what *commitment* means to you. Although it's a word we all know, we may not truly understand the full implications of a solid unwavering commitment to a marriage.

This aspect of commitment, the decision to stay married together, implies that when a couple faces a conflict, a dilemma, or an impasse, they have to reconsider carefully and caringly the initial stages of their love, that deep desire and promise to be together for life. The difficult part of the commitment is that it reminds us of that promise to *love* the other person under any circumstances for as long as we live. The promise to love includes honoring, cherishing, and respecting our mate. As we reconsider our promise, we assume the responsibility to perform every duty that a husband or wife owes to the spouse for life. In ignoring our romance days and the promises we made, we would miss that powerful human endowment of love that enables spouses to get through the hard times as well as the pleasant times.

Persons deeply in love and eager to get married tend to idealize their relationship. They have no accurate knowledge or concern about the background or personality of the individual they are going to marry. They trust their love and take it for granted that it will work in their married life. But marriage presents a significant number of hassles, demands to change lifestyle, accountability to each other, power struggles, and hard-to-deal-with conflicts. The more complex the partners' individual identities, the greater the challenges are likely to be. Couples with a mature attitude have a greater potential for weaving together a corporate marital identity, rich in variations and particularly attractive. It offers possibilities to meet basic, individual, emotional, physical, and spiritual needs in a deep and satisfying way. Such a union requires attention, flexibility, and respect on the part of both individuals. Their absence raises doubt that any couple would be able to sustain a healthy marital relationship.

I don't feel the same way as I did when we first fell in love, you may say. Very few people do. But we can recall the courting and romantic days, the promises of unconditional love, and the total surrender we made. You wanted this particular person in your life under any condition, and now you realize that you fell in love and married a human being and not an angel.

I often tell a bit about my marriage to clients who are facing marital problems; the story indicates that I also belong to the human race. Here's my story:

"When I decided to get married, there was only one angel around, so I married her."

They smile! Then I add what I told to my four married children when they faced initial difficulties.

Ultimately, every spouse proves to be a disappointment.

They do not want to hear that and they ask me, *Why?*

Because most of us marry our fantasies, thinking that all our needs will be met by the one we choose. But that's not reality. Now that your passion has subsided and you are facing the reality of married life, your spouse is no longer the angel you thought, and you may be asking, What happened to our love?

It is still there, but you cannot see it under the clouds of anger, just as you cannot see the sun behind the clouds. As your disappointment subsides, reality needs to be rediscovered. Are you willing to make an effort? Seriously reconsider the word commitment *before you answer the question, What happened to our love?*

Is it possible that you are willing to surrender to a process of reevaluating your married life once again and give it another chance?

Your answer may be, I have done that already. We went to different marriage therapists several times; I don't think it's going to work.

I can understand your hesitation, and it may seem easier to make a list of all your complaints, employ a lawyer, and go through divorce proceedings. If you are disappointed over your relationship or if you already have other plans in mind for your future, nobody can stop you. You made a decision. Other people have done it, you say to yourself.

But is it really a divorce that you want, or have you envisioned only a little contract between you and your spouse—a contract implying: You can have me now, dear love, as long as you take care of my needs and are good to me? If something bad happens to me, though, I'm going to take my commitment back. I can easily break our contract.

If you are facing serious problems, and struggles chip away at your initial promises bit by bit, you may need a seasoned marriage therapist to help you look deeper into yourself. Whether you believe or not, pray to God for guidance. God is a reliable source.

If married people kept their promises, not only would the divorce rate be reduced, but marriages would become significantly better. It is sad to see statistics and documents reporting the increasing divorce rate. People who are entering marriage or who are already married realize how difficult it is to make the marriage work. Every occupation in life except marriage requires training. With the exception of certain couples who attend premarital counseling classes, most marriages start with little preparation or training. Unequipped, individuals jump into married life, and they are shocked when difficulties surface. Why? Because everyone, especially the two partners, simply assumes they can have a successful marriage because of their great love, their passionate feelings, and past successes. This assumption is absurd, but it is the reason given by the overpowering confidence of naïve and unprepared marriage partners. Marriage is difficult, and if we do not face it realistically, the divorce rate is going to stay at epidemic levels. Building successful marriages is demanding and requires hard work and problem-solving skills.

Living in Difficult Relationships

It is not the institution of marriage that creates problems. It is, rather, the way that couples view their marriages and the manner in which they react toward each other that generates this condition. When you sense a little turbulence in your married life, there is no need to despair or wallow in self-pity or think that you have made a bad choice. This condition is self-created, and since it is self-created, it can be changed for the better no matter how long you have been married. Every couple has the personal power to re-create their marriage and transform it into the kind of loving relationship each partner desires.

Marriage is the one area in our times in which couples have total power to share their course for better or worse. As such, marriage should be considered a challenge instead of an insolvable problem, for it offers each of us the opportunity to make our relationship a priority, stretch our abilities, and use them more effectively than we have done previously.

If your current life is the worst ever, it is also the *best* for your marriage. Out of the critical period, your own inner wisdom will surface to guide you. Under the influence of anger, you may think of divorce, and who is the married person who can deny that this thought never crossed his or her mind? You hear statistics about the divorce rate. They vary from year to year; here is a sampling: 50 percent of all first marriages end in divorce. The remarriage rate is 70 percent, and 55 percent of these second marriages end in divorce. More than 80 percent of the remaining intact marriages are mildly or severely frustrated. Few of us know how to make a marriage work effectively. People whom you know, or even your own parents, may have gone through a divorce. It is a fact of our times, now an accepted fact of our life. The institution of marriage has been attacked as an outmoded institution. Young people in their early teens are sexually active; parents think of it as an inevitable reality and provide means for their children to avoid pregnancies. Couples in love agree to live together for a long while in order to test themselves and see if they would make suitable marriage partners. Can you imagine going to a dealership to buy a car and asking the salesperson if you could have this particular car for a couple of months to see if it is what you really want? If you find it satisfactory, you will oblige him by purchasing it. The salesperson may think you are from another planet. A realtor may respond in a similar fashion should you tell him you want to live in this house for six months or a year to test the plumbing, after which time you will decide whether to buy it or not. In my years of counseling couples, I have seen a large number of long-term relationships—of two, three, five, and more years—that have ended in separation.

There is no guarantee that a marriage will work if a couple lives together for a year or two as a test of compatibility. Many people do, and they persist in thinking that living together is the way to go. In some situations, it works, and eventually the couple gets married. Others walk away after a long-term relationship, leaving behind at least one broken heart. *Living together* before marriage implies personal insecurity, for the proponents of the idea are not fully aware of the transitions that we make in life and the transitory needs that all humans encounter.

There is only one guarantee that promises what would make a good marriage, and that is hard work. In any relationship where the other person—be it a spouse or a friend—appears difficult to us, we tend to forget that we may appear just as difficult to that other person. When we focus our attention on the significant other person, we have better success. It is a reality that either spouse, at one time or another, can be a difficult person, because each individual wants things done his or her way. All these aspects of human interaction are normal, but the sooner we realize that we cannot have things our way, the sooner we will be freer and happier.

If you do not wish to add another number to the divorce statistics, explore and develop the potential of your present marriage or your relationship. All aspects of your marriage cannot be bad; why not look deeper into your relationship? Many couples who value their vows and want to develop what appears to be the healthy side of the relationship seek a marriage therapist and engage in a therapeutic process that is based on hope and work. Others compulsively pursue a divorce in the fantasy that the next partner will make them happier, not necessarily realizing that they bring themselves, along with their personal baggage, into another relationship.

THOUGHTS TO CONSIDER:

- Accept the idea that you have made many choices in your life for personal reasons. Accept the fact that some of the choices you made did not serve your purpose, and probably hurt you emotionally and otherwise. Much frustration and pain comes from bad choices or unmet expectations. Now you are better equipped to make better choices.
- As you reexamine your relationship, take a positive look at your spouse, and recognize a place where a little construction or reinforcement is needed. You may build up your spouse, encourage a dialogue, and discover additional strength in the process. Be patient. Building of any kind takes a long time; you have to put up with many delays and inconveniences. Think and visualize the possibility of success.
- Be humble in your approach. Assertiveness has it place, but an aggressive approach to a relationship can be destructive. You are enormously important to your spouse. He or she knows it already. Surely there is fear that you may fail in your efforts to rekindle a loving relationship. How would you know if you do not make a concerted effort? Do your part as well as you can and trust in God for direction.
- As we advance in married life, each spouse has the tendency to focus on the weaknesses of the other. To maintain peace, we ignore these weaknesses or keep a mental record that we may use them against the other when dissatisfaction and frustration reach an unbearable point. Then when we explode we tear the other down. What if you develop another record and list the strengths of your relationship? You may discover that some good qualities and strengths outnumber the weaknesses.

- Life is too short to keep looking for weaknesses, finding molehills to build into mountains. This is true in anyone's marriage, being a union of two imperfect people. Each spouse wants to have his or her own way. Reality tells us that we cannot possibly have all our expectations met 100 percent.

CHAPTER 19

Spiritual Strength

Life is not always easy, but it can be ecstatic. To taste the ecstasy is the goal of any spiritual practice. Spiritual practices are so rewarding because they not only make us happier, but also ultimately open the door to bliss, a type of inner joy that is infinitely more profound and satisfying than any other of our usual fleeting pleasures.

Roger Walsh, MD, PhD

Every person has his or her own way of dealing with basic questions about self and about married life. *How did we get here in the first place? What is the marriage institution all about? What is my relationship to my spouse?* We want to know what the right answers are. We could explain some of this psychologically, but I do not think that provides the full picture. It is clear that some invisible power brings a man and woman together. For some, it may be the peak moment of physical attraction or the sexual search for fulfillment. To a believer, this power is God, who wants his creation of humans to continue. "*...male and female he created them. God blessed them, and God said to them, 'Be fruitful and multiply, and fill the earth...'*" (Gen 1:27–28).

If God and his power are part of our married life, we may have to apply biblical principles and admonitions to fulfill his will. Some of these basic principles are:

1. Love your partner as you love yourself.
2. Forgive the errors of your partner, as you would expect to be forgiven.
3. True love implies effort and emotional availability.
4. By being emotionally available and giving of yourself, you will receive love.
5. The closer you draw to God, the closer you will draw to your spouse.

God makes available an inner strength to all who seek him and follow his teachings. This power—God's power—not only helps us apply his principles but also helps and sustains the marital relationship when the going gets rough. It is God's power that gives us life, causes our lungs to breathe, our hearts to beat, and our bodies to grow and to move. His power can hold our marriage together and help it grow and be a source of joy.

A Biblical passage reassures us of God's love:

Beloved, let us love one another, because love is from God; everyone who loves is born of God and knows God. Whoever does not love does not know God, for God is love. (1 John 4:7–8)

God's power is manifested when two people truly love each other. God smiles when his children are happy. When partners work together to make their marriage a part of God's design and when they pray to him for guidance and strength, their love blossoms. This love not only sustains us and makes us God's cocreators as we bring children into his world, but it also helps us to make our way in the world and walk in the straight paths of righteousness.

I had the opportunity to counsel several couples of different religious orientations who encountered difficulties in their marriages. For many couples and their families, spirituality is crucial. For them, if spiritual concerns are ignored, the material world becomes confining. St. Paul brings to our attention what he calls *unseen warfare* in the spiritual realm. One force he interprets as our *natural desires*; the other force is the *Holy Spirit*. These two forces within us are constantly fighting each other to win control over us, and our wishes are never free of pressures (Gal 5:17). Have you ever experienced real anger or jealousy or even hate? Many married people experience these feelings. A battle is involved within most of us, and the winner is the person who turns to God and asks for help: *Lord, deliver me from this temptation and make known to me the path that I must follow today.* God knows our trouble, and the Holy Spirit who abides in each one of us helps us to regain inner peace. When this takes place it leads to a good life and a good marriage.

Many Christian couples have related similarities in how they maintain their own spiritual life. Often they have a small sanctuary neatly arranged in a special place in their home. Here is where they keep a Bible or cross or prayer book. This is their sacred place where they offer daily prayers. Emerging each day from home after prayer, they feel strong and ready to tackle their daily tasks. In the evening as they prepare to go to bed, some couples sit together and read a few verses from the Bible. This, they feel, is God's word for both of them. Sometimes they read and share their comments. At other times, they offer a prayer of thanksgiving to God for guiding them safely through the day, and they may ask God to give them a restful sleep.

While this model may be practical and worthwhile in some marriages, other married couples choose a different manner to connect with their creator, such as attending a church service together each Sunday. Shared spirituality may prove to be the strongest foundation for any marriage. When two people cling to each other, either in times of happiness or in crises, and pour their feelings out to God, they trust that there is a merging and blending that weaves them together.

The world we live in every day, what we call the material world, largely involves our external wellness—that which is outside our skin. If we have a good marriage that focuses on material things, after initial happiness, we are likely to be deeply disappointed. Spirituality involves what is inside each person. It is built around a quest for a deeper meaning of life. It provides an inner and more lasting joy. Couples who share their experiences, thoughts, feelings, concerns, and involvements in developing a spiritual identity tend to hold together and become healthier and happier than those couples who do not.

When you and your spouse take a few minutes each day to offer a prayer wherever you happen to be, spiritually you are processing and forging a life together. When speaking to your Lord God, either alone or together, in your own words, feelings and hopes become the prayer that welds you together. Partners who develop their capacity to share their spiritual quests—consistently practicing their faith—are destined to have a better marriage. When you pray together, you stay together, and you overcome the greatest of all marital enemies—emotional distance.

In practicing your faith—living a Christian life, being compassionate, loving, and charitable—you will discover that there is a God whose love will nurture your love for your partner, and your partner's love for you, making your marriage an emotionally healthy and happy relationship. Bible classes, spiritual readings, participation in humanitarian projects, and involvement in missionary services help to further the wellness of the larger community. You feel much inner joy in being involved in a spiritual activity that your faith and efforts make possible.

In chapter 5 of his Letter to the Galatians, the apostle Paul indicates that a healthy spiritual search results in a person being guided by the Holy Spirit. When this happens, St. Paul says the individual becomes full of *love, joy, peace, patience, kindness, goodness, faithfulness, gentleness, and self-control.* Think how easy it would be to live with a person who demonstrates these qualities. The potential to demonstrate these qualities to others exists within you. When you were baptized, our Lord Jesus endowed you with the gift of the Holy Spirit. Now it is up to you to develop these qualities.

Aware of human frailties, St. Paul admits that all kinds of problems occur that create chaos in a marriage. Hostility, jealousy, and anger can consume your best efforts at establishing a good, loving marriage. Constant complaints and criticisms indicate that you feel everyone else is wrong and you are right, thereby weakening your relationship with your spouse. Think how these attitudes could wipe out your marriage!

Remember, the emotional and spiritual investments you make today in building a dream relationship for you and your partner will yield generous dividends. Think seriously about the kind of life they will provide for each of you individually and for the two of you together. When two people love each other and feel emotionally connected, they can derive a great deal of joy from their marriage. Hundreds of couples whose successful marriages I have observed seem to agree on the following points:

1. We will love each other under any circumstances for as long as we live.
2. We will search after meaning and satisfaction together.
3. We will support and encourage each other at every turn in life.
4. We will enable and help each other to attain our individual goals.
5. We will be involved in spiritual activities, serving others and participating in the community life of our faith.

Think of a dear friend whose marriage is now on the brink of breaking up. *What happened to their agreement?* you may ask. Although their intentions were genuine initially, they were not able to follow what they had promised to each other. If we believe that marriage is a divine institution designed by God for companionship and for procreation, then, unquestionably, spiritual sustenance was lacking. Inviting God to be present in your married life is good practice and adds a powerful dimension to your relationship.

In this book, one of the chapters raises the question, *What is this thing called love?* There is one Greek word that summarizes concepts for solid foundations for marriage and family. It is *agape*, the word that suggests unconditional love. It is Godly love. Regardless of how long you are married, you may redefine agape, meaning *love*, as a willful commitment to give to your partner without expecting to get anything in return. Remove expectations as you do things for your mate, and you will notice that you feel free, and your heart overflows with loving feelings, leaving no room for disappointment. Even if you have thoughts about divorce, rest assured that agape will encourage you to carry your marriage through the most adverse times. You can make a conscious commitment never to stop giving to your mate. You can be the tree that grows daily and yields blossoms and fruits according to the seasons. In spite of major obstacles, with love and respect you can give yourself to your mate in the pursuit of marital harmony.

A sure way to feel stronger in loving your mate is to submit your marriage to God's law. God will unconditionally unleash the power within you, which will help you to choose, willfully, to love your mate. Remember, love is not simply a feeling; it is a conscious decision, a willful act of which you are in charge. God commands us to love one another because he knows we can appropriate love and receive its reward. Pray daily to God for the power to love your spouse. Promise God that you will give the *love that never ends* (1 Cor 13:8). The apostle Paul advises:

> Do nothing from selfish ambition or conceit, but in humility regard others as better than yourselves. Let each of you look not to your own interests, but to the interests of others. (Phil 2:3–4)

Can you see yourself putting your mate's needs ahead of your own? That is a difficult task. Think of the possibility of pushing aside your own needs for a while and wanting to please your mate. You may be thinking, *What if my mate does not deserve special treatment?* It is possible. Then giving love becomes a challenge for you. Agape motivates us to give to an imperfect person—yes, even to an undeserving person. Remember, your goal is to strengthen your marriage.

It is easy to become disillusioned after giving and giving without reciprocity, not even a thank-you. Agape does not require love in return. Love does not give in order to get. True love is a warm feeling in the presence of your partner, a loyal sense of devotion. God created man and woman with a unique need to belong to each other. God looked at all he had created and saw that "*it was very good*" (Gen 1:31). But when God looked at Adam, He saw something was missing. "*Then the Lord God said, 'It is not good that the man should be alone; I will make him a helper as his partner'*" (Gen 2:18).

Obviously Adam was lonely. God prescribed the love of companionship to fill Adam's loneliness. God gave Adam a woman, Eve, to love, cherish, and enjoy. This need to belong cannot be met by any other person, whether mother, father, sister, brother, or intimate other; it can be met only by your mate, the one that you chose to be your life's partner: "*Therefore a man shall leave his father and mother and be joined to his wife, and the two shall become one flesh*" (Matt 19:5).

Being a married couple, both of you have a home in each other's hearts—a safe place where you can find warmth and shelter from the storms of life. You belong to each other. In the Song of Solomon, the Shulamite bride expresses the love of belonging she shares with her mate when she says, "*I am my beloved's and my beloved is mine*" (Sol 6:3). "*Love one another with mutual affections, outdo one another in showing honor*" (Rom 12:10). Reach out and touch your mate. Hug each other warmly in the morning. Sit close together at home or in the car. Reach over and lovingly hold hands. An old myth tells of King Midas, whose touch turned everything into gold. In marriage, the loving touch turns everything into love. God wants us to be loving; he wants to see us happily married. Romance is part of a loving relationship that initiates married life. God gives us a beautiful book, the Song of Solomon, which describes romantic love in marriage. The Bible describes the love Jacob had for Rachel: "*So Jacob served seven years for Rachel, and they seemed to him but a few days because of the love he had for her*" (Gen 29:20).

Only romantic love could make seven years seem like a few days. Jacob was euphoric; he was on cloud nine. He was high on love. Truly, romantic love is real and you need to share it with your mate. Most wives have little trouble understanding eros; quite often they are starving for romance. Some husbands tend to ignore romance after marriage, although during their courting period, they are passionate and romantic.

If you are honestly serious about strengthening your marriage, project a warm, positive attitude toward your mate. Kindness goes a long way toward developing a warm climate for romance. Since love is sensitive to sight and scent, your grooming, or the lack of it, can turn your mate on or off. Be clean. If you want to get close to your mate, make sure you are appealing. Wives, keep your hair neat and pretty. Husbands, shave those whiskers; it is difficult to go cheek to cheek with a cactus. Practice personal hygiene and use a little cologne or perfume to spice things up. Dress neatly, even when you are relaxing around the house. Wives, dress as appealingly as possible for your husband. Husbands, dress to please your wife. Find out what your mate likes to see you in and then aim to please.

Couples who are in love look at one another. The eye is the mirror of love. Create a romantic climate with your mate through eye contact. Look warmly into your mate's eyes when you talk. In public places look for your mate, catch his or her eye and smile or wink. You will be sending the message *I love you* from your eyes to your mate's heart. "*You have ravished my heart with a glance of your eyes*" (Sol 4:9).

Our pressures in life often cause distance; we become busy, tired, cold, and aloof. A kiss has always been the symbol of affection and warmth. Make kissing the official form of greeting your mate. In the morning, a kiss is a pleasant way to start the day. A kiss at any time during the day is an excellent way to sustain your mate's love. When you reunite in the evening, greet each other with a kiss. When you are about to go to sleep, bring the day to a close with a kiss. It is amazing how a little evidence of love, like a kiss, can promote a good spirit in your married life. *Little things mean a lot.* In no other area of marriage can so little mean so much. Don't ever stop doing little things for your mate, especially kissing.

THOUGHTS TO CONSIDER:

- The strongest and safest foundation on which to build or reconstruct a marriage or a relationship is with God, the Giver of Life. A firm faith in the Creator and Sustainer of the world, who keeps the universe in harmony, can sustain, remodel, and harmonize your life.
- Wherever your life is today, you are seeking ways to improve your situation and be happier. If you are looking only for the attainment of material goods to make

you feel happy and at peace, you are setting yourself up for disappointment. After the initial excitement of the attainments, you will be searching for new sources and will never be truly satisfied or happy.

- No matter who you are or where you are in life, your basic need is the same as any other person's. The need consists of a life of essence and meaning, and an experience in which you sense the ever-presence of God, that inconceivable power who brought you to life and continues to keep you alive.

- The flick of an electrical switch floods a dark room with light. The power of electricity makes it possible and makes our lives more pleasant and brighter. Likewise, the power of God, who sustains this infinite universe and makes life possible, can enrich and brighten your personal and your married life.

- At this point in your life, regardless of the struggles you have faced or are still facing, you may discover new and more fulfilling ways of living. It has happened to others, and it can happen to you when you get involved with your faith. Whether it be a church or a temple or a mosque, when you start participating actively, you will notice the difference in your thoughts, feelings, and behavior.

- When you connect with God, within a few moments of prayer your frowns may turn into smiles, and you may sense a feeling of belonging. We are all God's people; we live in his world, and he is our Father. He loves us unconditionally, gives us life, wants us to be happy, heals the sick, brings comfort to those who suffer, and reforms the sinners.

- Each prayer we offer, regardless of its simplicity, reacquaints us with God's purpose in our life. Regular prayer is a source of strength derived from Almighty God. Our physical self, in addition to requiring healthy nourishment and exercise, needs oxygen to survive. The unseen part of us, our spiritual self, requires prayer for its nourishment and sustenance.

Epilogue

When I began to write *Living in Difficult Relationships*, my wife Pat looked at me with a curious smile and said, "You're not planning to write about us, are you?" "Of course not," I said. "We have a perfect marriage!" We embraced each other and laughed, admitting the realities of married life. I'm sure that there must have been times when she viewed me as a difficult person, and maybe I was. At other times, I may have seen her as difficult. Like any other married couple, we shared difficulties, but we did not run away. We tried to override the waves and make better choices. We sought opportunities that created positive changes toward a shared life worth living.

There is no perfect marriage. Many people find it difficult to see life with a spouse as a human relationship that requires effort and hard work. There are a few characteristics in every human being that may not change. If you are dealing with your spouse or with a live-in partner who is not willing to cooperate, regardless of how you feel about the relationship, you need to decide if you are willing to learn to live with that person.

Some time ago, I heard a story about a man who was passionate about his landscape. Pruned bushes, azaleas, and manicured grass made his front yard look like a postcard. There were spots of crabgrass on his lawn, however. He wrote to the Department of Agriculture in his state to find out how to cope with the crabgrass that spoiled his otherwise perfect lawn. The department responded with a number of suggestions. The man tried the suggested anti-crabgrass treatments without results. Summer came and his front lawn was still riddled with crabgrass. Exasperated, he wrote to the department again, noting that every method they had suggested had failed. The Department of Agriculture replied in a brief note: "We suggest that you learn to live with it."

Sometimes we need to learn how to live with the imperfections in our life. Truly, love, romance, financial security, and comfortable living make life easier for couples but do not guarantee perfection, because marriage consists of imperfect partners. A good married life does not come by chance but by choice. Each spouse brings into the relationship a unique contribution and each day comes full of new possibilities. We are confronted with two choices: we can take a profound look within, learn not to blame the other, and assume equal responsibility for our relationship, or we can run away from the difficult spouse.

My hope is that this book brings awareness and hope during a critical time in your marriage. Most likely you have discovered your own strength and the wisdom to reconnect with your spouse with a positive attitude. You probably have become aware of workable ideas that could be your own springboard toward a better relationship with the same partner.

It's too late, you may say. I'm already out of the house and have consulted a lawyer. I know what I'm doing. I have even found a new love, somebody who truly adores me, and I have decided that my life will be far better with her as a companion. It looks like a pleasant dream! The grass may look greener elsewhere, but is it? It may surprise you to learn that human conflict, *if properly managed,* can be a transforming and stabilizing vehicle to make any relationship vibrant and healthy. In every person there is work to be done. In every marriage there are issues that need attention. In every human heart is the potential to do what needs to be done. Return to the one that you loved and married, begin life again where you left off, and make it better. Any time to start is a good time.

I am grateful you have allowed this book to be your companion on your journey toward a better relationship. My hope is that the road map I have designed will give you clear directions and new possibilities.

Appendices

Human Sexuality

> As soon as the gates of successful love have been opened, there will always remain in the depth of the lovers' hearts an ardent hope for further adventures for deeper excursions in the garden of sex. The pleasure itself, being both immense and insufficient, gives rise to ever-increasing desire for lovemaking.
>
> José de Vinck

Now that you have reviewed the principles of love, you are ready to consider another important, sensitive, and sacred area to enhance your married life: the art of sexuality. Lack of understanding of human sexuality causes distance and in many cases divorce between two loving people. The Creator designed sex for the continuation of his creation. Without sex, you and I would not be here. Sex, as a part of human life, is inseparable from our personhood. Human life is good. Personhood is good. So sex is good. It was created to pursue expression in loving relationships that enrich and enhance life. Sex is powerful and touches life at its very core. Sex is more than physical thrills; it is an emotional, a psychological, and even a spiritual experience. The sex act requires a deep commitment to mutual responsibility and well-being. Male and female sex organs need each other to be completed. Sex is designed to be shared, giving and receiving, loving and being loved, completing and being completed.

The act of sexual intercourse between two people is, in itself, beautiful and good. Almost all religious systems maintain great reverence for sexuality and its place in marriage. For this reason, our society is becoming increasingly concerned that young people become more responsible for their sexuality. *Doin' what comes naturally* may not be a good guide for your sexual life. Lovemaking is a learned activity, and it takes willing partners to master the skills of sexuality. There is a mysterious dimension in our human sexuality, a forceful attempt to become one with the other. *And the two shall be one flesh,* claims the Bible. Once this oneness is attained, lovemaking leaves us feeling rewarded, and yet not totally. We feel complete, yet incomplete, because we want more pleasure. Human nature is always pleasure-seeking. In this process, the search for more satisfaction continues as we discover each other's sexual potential.

One issue that merits writing another chapter is the issue of human insatiability. To some extent most men and women suffer from the malady of insatiability, meaning that regardless of how much of everything they have, it is not enough. This common desire of wanting more surfaces surreptitiously in a sensitive area: lovemaking.

In their effort to have a more satisfying sexual experience, most couples fail to confront human nature's insatiable desire—be it for love, sex, attention, money, fun, recognition, food, material possessions, security—that cannot be supplied in sufficient quantities to satisfy this deep yearning completely. In reality both genders have equally insatiable natures, and they often share areas of insatiability.

Men desire sexual variety. After having a wonderful lovemaking experience with his loving wife, a husband may see a sexy woman and may instantly desire that woman as if he had not had sex in a month. His urge has no memory. It is important that his mind reminds him of his commitment to marriage and that his loving woman is back at home.

Women desire emotional intimacy. If a woman had a delightful, intimate weekend in an exotic resort alone with her husband, upon their return home, as soon as they face the reality of domestic and work-related responsibilities, her desire for intimacy may make her think that intimacy is lacking in their marriage.

Although they feel sexually satisfied with their partner, many men lust for another partner. Part of this desire for men is socially induced. It can characterize women as well. Most of us are aware that the multibillion-dollar pornography industry is entirely male oriented—and it offers an endless supply of new lust objects. Even one issue of *Playboy* will suffice to confirm that male nature is variety oriented. Because of this, the male is mainly visual, easily influenced by seeing an attractive female, whom he does not even know, and having sexual fantasies about her. The female is more emotional; she is easily influenced when she is treated with kindness, sensitivity, generosity, and genuinely complimented. She may feel a tinge of jealousy when she sees another man treating his wife like a queen. Interacting with a handsome male, a woman may have some fantasies: *How would I feel if I were his partner?* While women may have an insatiable urge for attention, God has endowed them with the ability to control, and this control behaves in the opposite manner of that of the male urge. If women were possessed to the same degree as the male with the yearning to have many partners, the world would self-destruct—marriage would be obsolete, and men and women would waste their lives amid lust and sexually transmitted diseases.

Lest the above male or female description be misunderstood, I would like to caution the reader that it is only offered to describe an area of vulnerability: being insatiable can be destructive in any significant relationship, especially in marriage.

To combat this problem, men and women must acknowledge to themselves that both sexes have different natures and different areas of vulnerability. They must continually grapple with the fact that they can never satisfy their insatiable natures. Even in the best of circumstances—married to a loving spouse with whom they relate well—periodically couples will still have their own individual frustration. The thought that somewhere out there, either more exciting sex or emotional involvement can be attained is just a fantasy.

The moment a man or a woman thinks that sexual contentment is attainable by sleeping with another partner—*a particular "angel" who is a total mystery to them*—they are setting themselves up for trouble.

During this writing, Gabriel, a forty-six-year-old husband and father of two children felt attracted to a younger woman, Rita, an associate at work. She looked sexy to him and also sad. It did not take long for Gabriel to ask her what was wrong. She took the bait and soon he became her comforting confidant. Over a cup of coffee, she revealed that she and her husband were not getting along. In turn, Gabe, as he liked to be called, also shared his dissatisfaction with his wife. *She is a good woman and a good mother, but I have no more loving feelings for her.*

He found Rita a good listener, and their dialogues became longer each time they met. One day after work hours they decided to go for a drink to relax. The drink became dinner. After a few such intimate meetings, they went to a hotel and spent a few hours together. Their affair lasted for three months. Rita fell in love with Gabe and made demands on his time. Because she wanted to spend more time with him, she decided to divorce her husband. When Gabe heard this, he made himself unavailable. Angry that she kept calling him and threatening to call his wife, he no longer found her attractive. *"It's not going to work,"* he said emphatically and ended the affair. *There are other good-looking women out there,* he thought. *I can find someone to please me.*

Men and women will always be tempted. They will lust for someone new and exciting, although such attributes do not guarantee contentment. Knowing and understanding their insatiable natures and being able to control themselves can be liberating, and couples can find contentment in each other.

You may recall the earlier years of your marriage, when lovemaking was abundant. A strong desire for sexual intimacy and frequency was ever present. As time passed, this forceful passion waned. Nature returned to a more livable balance. What was a three-times-a-day experience was mutually reduced to three times a week, or even three times a month. For some couples, sex became a once-a-month experience.

This initial shift to sexual moderation often brings about one of the most serious marital crises: *What's wrong with you? Don't you love me any more? Am I not attractive to you any more? Are you seeing someone else? Oh, I'm too tired; just leave me alone.* Such questions and comments evoke familiar insecurities in each of the spouses, making them wonder: *Will I ever be able to satisfy my mate or myself?* Anxieties caused by personal insecurities could very well result in sexual dysfunctions. Physical or emotional illness definitely hinders sexual interest as well.

To transcend anxiety and anger, it is important to refute the prevailing myths that some of us believe:

1. **Sex is something a man does to a woman.**
   Incorrect. Sex is a shared experience. Each spouse facilitates the sexual act to attain pleasure and increase intimacy.
2. **Sex is a peak, intense ecstasy when you are in love.**
   Sex is always helpful after you have had an argument.
3. **The size of your partner's organ guarantees satisfaction.**
   Easily inflated; easily deflated. What brings satisfaction to sexual experience is not size. It is the caring for each other's needs and the tenderness in the process—known as emotional involvement with one another—that brings physical fulfillment.
4. **The frequency of sex indicates intimacy.**
   Not necessarily, although some couples may perceive it that way. Intimacy is a state of grace. It is the ability to be with your spouse for long periods of time without feeling that you have to perform for his or her entertainment. Your spouse is your partner in most aspects of your life, a person with whom you can share joys and sorrows, concerns and ambitions. He or she is not there as a sexual object to satisfy sexual drives.
5. **Sex is initiated by the man.**
   The woman must remain passive lest she be accused of being promiscuous or experienced. Or: *Sex is initiated by the woman.* In reality, both statements are incorrect. In a good marriage, either the man or the woman may initiate lovemaking. As in other aspects of married life, the sexual relationship should not be all one person's responsibility.
6. **All physical contact should lead to sex.**
   In a healthy relationship, a hug and a kiss start and end the day. It is a validation of the other, an acceptance that this other is most important in one's life. When a wife complains, *Each time he touches me, he wants sex,* she indicates there is a problem. She feels used, not loved. Truly, a male may be eas-

ily stimulated, but does he have to make love each time he hugs or kisses his wife? It may be more rewarding to give each other physical affection—a back rub, a massage—as a gift with no further expectation.

7. **A satisfactory sex life indicates that the marriage is good. A poor sexual relationship is a major cause of marriage failure.** There is no doubt that bedroom bliss overflows into most areas of married life. It is not enough to rate high only on sexual performance; domestic responsibilities must not be ignored. Unsatisfactory sex is a symptom, not the cause, of marital discord. Your perception of what represents a good sexual relationship is more important than the sex act itself.

8. **If you and your spouse don't climax at the same time, something is missing.** What is missing is the awareness of male and female sexuality. Mutual orgasm may be enjoyable, but it is neither necessary nor always achievable. Male and female experiences consist of different rates of arousal. The man becomes visually excited and can reach climax more quickly than a woman. A woman needs to be emotionally ready to receive her counterpart. She needs more stimulation. Here is where foreplay is imperative. So, while mutual orgasm is desirable, in most situations it is the exception rather than the rule. Rest assured that separate orgasms are just as satisfying as simultaneous orgasms.

9. **Sex must be performed in a certain way.** Sexual standards established by advertising, literature, soap operas, plays, and television programs have brainwashed people into the belief that sex should be performed in a certain way. This is misleading information. There is no *normal* sexual performance; lovemaking varies greatly from one marriage to another, both in quality and quantity. Family therapists follow the rule: Treat the relationship before you focus on the sexual problem. This rule is based on the premise that the sexual relationship mirrors the whole relationship between partners. What happens outside the bedroom in day-to-day interaction has a tremendous influence on what happens inside the bedroom.

10. Women have lower sex drives than men.

Research indicates that the female sex drive may be slightly higher than a man's. What seems to be ignored is the fact that a woman during one act of sexual intercourse may have several orgasms while the man may have only one.

The art of lovemaking is a process that includes new discoveries and delightful surprises. It takes time and effort, especially when we have to combat our society's bombardment of misinformation. As you bring each day to an end in your bedroom, look at your spouse as the most important person in your life. Each of you is unique, and each time you are ready to make love, feel the uniqueness of the experience; focus on pleasuring the other. It is in the giving of yourself that you receive the bliss of sexuality.

Timing is very important. Select the time when you both feel comfortable, relaxed, and psychologically ready. If you are undergoing stressful times—financial worries, in-law conflicts, career problems—lovemaking can wait. Sometimes physical fatigue or illness prevents you from sexual fulfillment. Your goal in the early years, as well as for the rest of your married life, is to be able to read the indicators accurately and to discuss the problems in terms of finding solutions. It is easy to assume that sex is the problem when, in fact, it is only reflecting other worries and tensions. As you become more aware that your sex life is interwoven with other areas of your personal and psychological development, you will be able to predict and avoid potential obstacles. The following questions may assist you as you seek to solve marital problems.

1. Do you feel that there is sufficient physical exchange with your partner, including touching, hugging, and kissing?
2. Are you pleased with your personal participation in lovemaking? What improvements would you like to make?
3. Does you partner know what your expectations are in your sexual activity? Are you willing to tell him or her what you expect?

4. Is your partner's interest in sex different from yours? Are you comfortable discussing and, possibly, resolving the differences?
5. Can you maintain a dialogue with your partner about your sexuality? Would you be able to accept your partner's opinion if it differs from your own?
6. Since the sexual act requires sensitivity from both partners, can you ask your partner for what you want in lovemaking?
7. When something thrilling happens as you make love, can you tell your partner about it? What if something disappointing happens?
8. Do you feel comfortable initiating sex? Do you initiate it half the time?

These are truly sensitive as well as difficult questions. As you and your spouse answer the above questions, make sure to respect each other's perceptions about human sexuality. When you have identified the specific aspects of lovemaking you wish to change, you are halfway to a solution. Try not to read each other's mind. Raise the questions and be willing to accept the fact that there might be more than one answer to each one.

Maintain the afterglow after lovemaking:

1. Help your spouse to reach satisfaction.
2. Ask your spouse to help you reach satisfaction.
3. Express love and tenderness after intercourse.
4. Give each other sufficient time together after intercourse. Relax, play soft music, take a nap together.
5. Tell your partner how much you have enjoyed the lovemaking experience. Mention aspects that you really liked and aspects that need to improve. Be careful that you don't become judgmental.

The challenges to satisfactory lovemaking apply to yourselves and other couples as well. The husband should understand, even when he gets older, that he must never stop courting and wooing his wife. A woman's love and her subsequent sexual response are not something a husband should take for granted. They are not things that a man should demand or things that a wife can force. Lovemaking is something that has to be earned continually and won more or less repeatedly.

Some men make the mistake of assuming that once they are married, their spouse will be constantly available and respond happily to sexual advances any time, under any conditions, and without any preparation. Most women are not made that way, no matter how much they love their husbands. A woman with a demanding husband might decide to try, but her feelings and body will refuse to cooperate. If a husband wants a happy wife and a warm receptive sexual partner, he has to become an expert in the art of sexuality—of preparing his wife emotionally and then physically for lovemaking.

Start by creating a climate of love for the woman. The husband needs to be consistent with his affections. He should not create a hot and cold relationship; he should not bring flowers and presents one day and make degrading remarks the next. Instead, he should show his wife an abiding love, so that she always knows where she stands.

In this love, there must be provision for her instinctive love needs and her special human needs. With the instinctive love needs, she has to feel precious, secure, and valued. She needs to know that she comes first in his life. Her special human needs are for friendship, affection, and romance. She must know that she is her husband's best friend, not someone he calls on when there is no one else interesting around, but the one he prefers to be with all the time if he has his choice. If he can provide for her needs and produce this comfortable climate; then, from this point of view, lovemaking becomes regular, frequent, and pleasurable.

Wives, too, have to learn the art of sexuality. Sex is not something that a man does to a woman or a woman does for the man. Human sexuality is God's gift to humans; it has a purpose and a time, and it needs to be treated carefully. Sexuality is more pleasurable and increases intimacy when it is mutually shared. Many women tend to neglect sex in the childbearing and caring stage. Some make time for lovemaking, and others take sex for granted and are satisfied with limited or no sex. *It's no longer important to me. I've had enough.* As a man becomes older, he becomes more of a gourmet and connoisseur in his sexual acts.

167

The quality of lovemaking tends to be more important as the quantity becomes less so. It is important that a wife responds to this change, that she accepts more responsibility for keeping this relationship fresh and exciting by using her imagination and putting forth special effort.

It is a good idea for the wife at times to take the initiative in sex. She has to figure out what it is that she likes best in lovemaking and pave the way by letting her husband know. A real guide for a husband has to be the wife's responses and reactions. She should communicate how she feels about his pace and manner—whether he is going too fast or is rough or is applying too much pressure or should move his hand just a little to the right. These are fairly simple pieces of information to pass back and forth. If all is going well and there is nothing to say, the wife can at least purr, and her husband will catch on very quickly.

It should be understood that making sexual intercourse mutually satisfactory is not the total responsibility of the husband. The wife has an active part to play as well. It is up to her to make sure there is a place in her life for making love. She cannot inundate her daily life with endless hours of work and unfinished tasks. It is of importance for both husband and wife to appropriate special time for romance and lovemaking.

Choosing or arranging the right time and place is imperative. If the agreement is to make love, all external things should be blocked out. You cannot be ready physically and mentally for lovemaking when you start discussing remodeling the house or looking for a new carpet for the living room or buying a new car. As important as these issues may appear, they can wait. After choosing a time and place, begin lovemaking with foreplay.

Foreplay should be a two-way street, with both partners feeling free to do what comes naturally to them and what gives pleasure to both of them. With a little extra effort, the wife will reach the stage of intense desire and will be willing and eager to go on with lovemaking.

Many men and women think that foreplay is a nuisance for men, an unavoidable delay. Some men delay as little as possible; they are eager to get on to the main event. This haste makes the woman feel inadequate and puts her under a lot of pressure, especially if she feels her spouse is timing her with a stopwatch. Foreplay should not be considered a nuisance, something to be rushed through quickly to get on to more enjoyable things. It should not be considered a *labor* of love; no one ever calls it work. It is called *play* and should be considered as play and as fun.

Trial and error, practice and experience, make foreplay rewarding. It requires cooperation, intelligence, patience, and honesty—and certainly a sense of humor to get out of tight corners. It is an art, something that has to be learned. Foreplay involves both style and time, and above all, it requires imagination, sensitivity, and lightness of touch. The rule here is: the more sensitive the area the lighter the touch must be.

In all areas of life, husband and wife teach each other. Here in particular, the wife is the teacher, and so it is important for her to remember that, basically, the student is not always too bright. Thus the wife must be prepared to be gracious, loving, and understanding with her partner's inevitable miscalculations.

The wife may snuggle next to her husband because she needs his warmth and affection, or because she is not feeling well, or because she's had an emotional setback and needs reassurance that she is loved. The husband may misinterpret her movements and assume that she is seeking lovemaking. Under these conditions, the wife needs to communicate her true feelings and avoid misleading her husband.

Another sensitive aspect of lovemaking is the afterglow. Some husbands, for some strange reason, after both have reached orgasm, stop dead in their tracks and have no further contact with their wives. Many even appear indifferent to their wives after their fulfillment, and others fall asleep. This behavior is very unsettling to the wife, because her instinctive love needs are threatened. *What am I? An object of pleasure?*

This period of afterglow need not be any more than just lying in each other's arms or next to each other holding hands, touching, and catching one's breath. Some couples may or may not even feel like talking. The important thing is that it is a time of peace and contentment when both can feel secure, safe and, above all, sure—sure of each other's love and sure of the permanency of love. In today's world there are few places and few times when you can feel certainty about anything, and this is one reason why you should use this time to the fullest.

Being a marriage and family therapist, I hear amazing stories in which husbands and wives treat each other like objects instead of persons. If you and your spouse are serious about treating each other like persons, you will make each other's needs your priority. If you fail to meet your spouse's needs, reality has a way of coming home to roost. When needs are not met at home, a spouse will look elsewhere for satisfaction; Satan stands by, ready to inject his venom of temptation. To make your marriage divorce-proof, consider the following:

All marriages revolve around a short but very big word: needs. Husbands and wives have basic but not similar needs that need to be met. Men and women both want great sex and warm affection. Generally speaking, men want more sex and women desire more affection, but the reverse can also be true. Women want their husbands to recognize their needs. The typical wife seldom gets enough hugs; she can always use another hug. A warm embrace and a kiss before you start your day can really send the day in a happy direction. Too often we underestimate the power of a kiss, a kind word, a smile, and a touch. The smallest act of caring has the potential to make your marriage stronger.

APPENDIX 2

Tools for Building a Better Marriage

A good marriage is a warm *fireplace*. The love that two people have for each other generates a warm place. But the warmth it creates does not warm just the two people in love; it warms everyone else who comes near them—their children, their neighbors, their community, and everyone who meets them.

Ronald Rolheiser

Most marriages succeed in becoming happier and more productive as a result of good attitudes on the part of both partners. An attitude consists of thoughts that are manifest in behaviors for everyone to see. What we privately think in our minds and what feelings we experience in our hearts eventually come out in the form of words, facial expressions, and behavior—all of which affect relationships. We have often heard the comment, *That one needs to get a new attitude!* We know that the remark means, *That person has a bad attitude.* Most of us understand that attitudes reveal character. Love, joy, peace—qualities of a happy life—can only be attained by good and positive attitudes; a bad attitude can only deprive us of such potential.

If you want to attract a human honeybee—a friend or a mate or a spouse—you may have to be a flower—not just a beautiful flower but one that also has nectar, a sweet essence, claims Bhante Y. Wimala. One may be a physically gorgeous-looking person, but if the inside is ugly and empty, he or she will attract only superficial attention. A bee, for example, does not seek the appearance of a flower; rather, it knows the sweetness is in the essence. For a human being, love, respect, and spirituality constitute the nectar of life, the sweet essence within.

Making a habit of having a good and positive attitude will change our life. As we focus carefully on the following tools and apply them with sensitivity, we can develop a better marriage.

1. **Develop a daily attitude of gratitude.**

   Show actively to each other your appreciation for both small and big things. Having positive feelings prevents a couple from taking each other for granted. It is not by accident that you met, fell in love, and decided to make a life together. Something sacred and special brought you together; honor, nurture, and cherish that feeling.

2. **Become friends.**

   A major ingredient of a good marriage is friendship. Become each other's best friend. Eat, sleep, walk, work, play, plan, and travel—perform all these activities with the one who provides your emotional, physical, and spiritual support.

3. **Make your mate feel loved.**

   Show your spouse every day—by frequently verbalizing— how much you love him or her, how glad you are when you are in his or her presence, and how wonderful it will be to spend a lifetime together. Do something or offer something that will please your spouse.

4. **Look at the positive qualities of your mate.**

   It's easy but dangerous to focus on the negative aspects of your marriage or of your partner. Be wise, sensitive, and caring enough to count your blessings. Talk about the strengths and good qualities of your mate.

5. **Develop a real partnership.**

   Having a working relationship with your spouse can be an incredible asset to the relationship. Working together cooperatively—whether the tasks are connected with your home, your children, your career, your church, or your future—will strengthen your marriage.

6. **Have realistic expectations.**

There are ups and downs in life. Maintain careful control over your expectations. High and elaborate expectations can be troublesome. Love and support each other even through difficult times. Use unmet expectations as the source of valuable lessons—discipline, self-control, and acceptance.

7. **Be accountable.**

Learn to inform your partner of personal or familial issues. A major decision should be based on the opinions of both partners. Input usually triggers good ideas. Your commitment to one another implies that each of you will contribute to your ultimate well-being and happiness.

8. **Manage disagreements.**

Small and large disagreements or conflicts occur in relationships. Therefore, it is important to develop a workable model to solve problems constructively. Simple ways include the following:

   a. Use good timing: Try not to discuss/debate/argue when you are tired.

   b. Use a gentle disclaimer when the issue to be discussed is serious. For example, his/her mother frequently stops at your home unannounced, and this bothers you. A good way to handle the mother-in-law issue is to say, *I love seeing your mother, but would you please ask her to give us a call before she drops in?*

   c. Use diplomacy and sensitivity. Every fall, your father-in-law comes to your house to clean the gutters. Your wife is happy to see him, but you are not. He is an older man and could easily fall off the roof. You could easily avoid hurting your wife's feelings by saying, *It's very generous of your father to clean our gutters, but it's risky climbing those ladders. We really must hire someone to do the job. Ask your father to come and join us for lunch.*

9. **Respect each other's uniqueness.**

Each spouse is a separate person. Thoughts, actions, and aspirations may not necessarily be common to both spouses. As long as it is not opposing or offending, freedom of expression ought to be encouraged. Freedom of action, provided that it does not endanger the relationship or disrupt interaction with others, should also be supported.

10. Be the architect of your marriage.

Although both of you are aware of the better qualities of the marriages of your parents and friends and you may wish to emulate them, it would serve your best interests to design and develop your own model. Your style of life does not have to please every relative or friend. It suffices that your lifestyle pleases you and God.

11. Keep nurturing your love.

You may have to pay special attention to each other's needs as they emerge. It is imperative to reach out to hug and kiss and say *I love you*. This behavior is important at any time of the day, and it makes the couple look forward to being together. Make it a priority to keep your love fresh and alive by being emotionally and physically present in your partner's life.

12. Make prayer a part of your daily life.

In your own words express thanks and gratitude to God the Giver of all blessings. Ask for his divine guidance in all aspects of your life: goal setting, decision making, parenting, conflict resolution, financial planning, and all of the everyday challenges. Pray and trust in his abundant love and divine providence.

The Marriage Creed

Agape is the only word that describes God's unconditional love for humanity. *Agape*, translated as *love*, came into being when Christ entered the world. When we ask, "What is *agape*?" it is like asking, "What is God?" Our finite minds cannot easily comprehend its meaning. *Agape* is the essence of life and life itself is a mystery. It is God himself whose creative energy sustains and propagates life. It cannot be forced upon anyone—it must come from the heart, and it is given to others as God's gift to be shared.

Irene, translated as peace, is Christ himself. The prophet Isaiah called him the Prince of Peace. The peace that Christ offers surpasses human understanding, and it comes to us as we attune our life with God's will. *Irene* is harmony in personal relations untroubled by conflict, agitation, or commotion. When Christ is present in our life, we have inner peace. His teachings guide us to love, forgive, heal, and reach out to all people regardless of their social status or personal condition. He enters our world to reassure us that we are sons and daughters of a loving God.

Read this Marriage Creed in the spirit of *agape and irene*. These two words meaning *love* and *peace* form acronyms for the paragraphs that follow.

Accept each other. Allow space in your heart to accommodate the person you have chosen and married. Your spouse is different from you; learn to accept his or her differentness.

Greet each other every day with a kiss and a feeling of belonging. You belong to each other; learn to care about your spouse. Each contact you make goes beyond the touching of the body. It is a touch of the inner world, your psyche.

Although you belong to each other as a husband-and-wife team, allow the other to be an individual. Allow him or her to grow and mature. Attempt not to make your spouse like yourself. He or she does have a self that needs to be nurtured and developed.

Preserve the purpose of marriage. Marriage is a close, intimate relationship in which two people share life on a very broad basis and in great depth. It is a partnership in which you and your spouse run a joint home, manage your money, share the responsibility of raising children, and establish relationships with relatives, friends, and neighbors.

Express your feelings to each other. A daily dialogue with your spouse helps in the understanding of each other's needs. Learn to listen so that you may understand the other. If you are listening for the sake of argument, you are not listening with your heart.

Involve yourself intelligently with your spouse. Becoming involved implies that each of you crosses the frontier that separates the two of you, and each enters, to some extent, the private life of the other, thereby gaining the spirit of mutual intimacy.

Respond to each other, not as a punitive parent but as a loving mate—no judgment, evaluation, or criticism. You are equal partners. Learn to live with each other as equals, in mutual love, respect, and trust.

Enrich your daily life with something new and different. An unexpected compliment encourages self-confidence for the other. Whatever you do for your spouse—an effort to cooperate in a common chore, lending a hand, bringing something special home, touching or hugging—enriches your marriage. Cultivate the spirit of friendship. If your partner becomes your friend, your marriage becomes a more pleasant experience.

Never allow anyone outside of your marriage to define your relationship. When you learn to know, trust, and love your partner, you can define the style of your marriage. Once you become aware of who you are, what you are, and what you are not, then cultivate your own individuality. Help your spouse to do likewise. Build your own marriage.

Every person and every relationship changes constantly. It is how you experience yourself, both individually and in the marriage, that needs your attention. Experience yourself in the present. Be emotionally present to your spouse in the immediacy of the present.

In focusing on these two acronyms, AGAPE-IRENE, LOVE-PEACE, you may develop another creed, a personal one. Reality indicates that as humans we have limitations. Before any admonitions and wise counsel, we have to accept our limitations and work with them in mind to produce our own creed that works in our marriage. Start with loving one another and allow God to enrich this love in your life.

Bibliography

It is with gratitude that I acknowledge the following books that have provided for me insight and inspiration to write my own book. Anyone who is interested in family or relationship dynamics will find these books helpful.

Becker, Ernest. *The Denial of Death.* New York: Free Press, 1973.

Beecher, Willard and Marguerite. *Beyond Success and Failure.* New York: Simon and Schuster, 1975.

Dobson, James. *Love Must Be Tough.* Dallas: Word Publishing, 1996.

Chapman, Gary. *The Five Love Languages.* Chicago: Northfield Publishing, 2004.

De Vinck, José. *The Virtue of Sex.* New York: Hawthorn Books, 1996.

Kalellis, Peter M. *Restoring Relationships: Five Things to Try Before You Say Goodbye.* New York: Crossroad, 2001.

————. *Twenty Secrets for Healing Thoughts, Feelings, and Relationships.* New York: Crossroad, 2005.

Krantzler, Mel. *Creative Marriage.* New York: McGraw-Hill, 1981.

Leman, Kevin. *Keeping Your Family Together When the World Is Falling Apart.* Colorado Springs: Focus on the Family Publishing, 1993.

Ruben, Harvey L. *Super Marriage.* New York: Bantam Books, 1986.

green press
INITIATIVE

Paulist Press is committed to preserving ancient forests and natural resources. We elected to print this title on 30% post consumer recycled paper, processed chlorine free. As a result, for this printing, we have saved:

4 Trees (40' tall and 6-8" diameter)
2 Million BTUs of Total Energy
382 Pounds of Greenhouse Gases
1,722 Gallons of Wastewater
109 Pounds of Solid Waste

Paulist Press made this paper choice because our printer, Thomson-Shore, Inc., is a member of Green Press Initiative, a nonprofit program dedicated to supporting authors, publishers, and suppliers in their efforts to reduce their use of fiber obtained from endangered forests.

For more information, visit www.greenpressinitiative.org

Environmental impact estimates were made using the Environmental Defense Paper Calculator. For more information visit: www.papercalculator.org.